T0316645

The Teaching of History

Essays on the Teaching of History

By *F. W. MAITLAND*,
H. M. GWATKIN,
R. L. POOLE,
W. E. HEITLAND,
W. CUNNINGHAM,
J. R. TANNER,
W. H. WOODWARD,
C. H. K. MARTEN,
W. J. ASHLEY.

CAMBRIDGE, *at the University Press*, 1901.

CAMBRIDGE UNIVERSITY PRESS
Cambridge, New York, Melbourne, Madrid, Cape Town,
Singapore, São Paulo, Delhi, Mexico City

Cambridge University Press
The Edinburgh Building, Cambridge CB2 8RU, UK

Published in the United States of America by Cambridge University Press, New York

www.cambridge.org
Information on this title: www.cambridge.org/9781107644557

First published 1901
First paperback edition 2013

A catalogue record for this publication is available from the British Library

ISBN 978-1-107-64455-7 Paperback

PREFATORY NOTE.

THE Syndics of the University Press confided the oversight of this collection of Essays to Lord Acton and myself. An Introduction by Lord Acton was to have been included but his unfortunate illness prevented this part of the arrangement from being carried out. Professor Maitland, under circumstances which make our obligation to him the greater, has kindly written the Introduction.

I may be permitted to thank the contributors for kindness which has made the mechanical part which I have performed such a pleasant one.

W. A. J. ARCHBOLD.

CAMBRIDGE.
September, 1901.

CONTENTS.

viii   *Contents.*

INTRODUCTION.

THE following essays were to have been ushered into the world by Lord Acton. That he is unable to perform for them this good office will be deeply regretted both by their writers and by their readers. Of what he would have written only this can be said with certainty, that it would have added greatly to the value of this book. Still it is not apparent that these essays, proceeding from men who have had much experience in the teaching of history, imperatively demand any introduction. A few words about a matter of which the essayists have not spoken nor been called upon to speak, namely, about the history of the teaching of history in the English universities, are all that seem necessary, and may be suffered to come from one who can look at schools of history from the outside.

The tale need not be long, and indeed could not be long unless it became minute. The attempt to teach history, if thereby be meant a serious endeavour to make historical study one of the main studies of the universities, is very new. We can admit that it has attained the manly estate of one-and-twenty years and a little more. But not much more. Some of those who watched its cradle are still among us, are still active and still hopeful.

The university of Oxford, it is true, came by a professorship or readership of ancient history in times that we may well call

ancient, especially if we remember that only in 1898 did the
university of Cambridge permanently acquire a similar professorship.   But those ancient times were in some respects
nearer our own·than are some times that have intervened.   The
professorship at Oxford was established by William Camden in
1622 at the end of a life devoted to history, and the founder
numbered among his friends many eager and accomplished
explorers of the past: Selden and Ussher, Spelman and
Godwin, Savile and Cotton.   Much had been done for history,
and more especially for English history, in the age that was
closing: an age that had opened when Matthew Parker set
scholars to work on the history of the English church and was
in correspondence with the Centuriators of Magdeburg.   The
political and ecclesiastical questions which had agitated mankind had been such as stimulated research in unworked fields.
Learning had been in fashion, and much sound knowledge had
been garnered.

For a moment it seemed probable that Cambridge would
not long be outstripped by Oxford.   One of her sons, Fulke
Greville, Lord Brooke, who was murdered in 1628, founded or
endeavoured to found a readership of history, which would
have balanced Camden's foundation.   He sought to obtain
Vossius from Leyden, and obtained from Leyden Dorislaus as
an occupant for the chair.   After two or three lectures the
lecturer was in trouble.   His theme was Roman history and
he said somewhat of the expulsion of kings : a matter of which
it is not always safe to talk at large.   That he would take part
in trying an English king for treason he did not foresee, nor the
vengeance that followed, nor the public funeral in Westminster
Abbey, nor the exhumation of bones that polluted a royal
sanctuary.   What at the present moment concerns us more is
the loss of an annuity that Lord Brooke meant, so it seems, to
be permanent.   Apparently our historians have as yet found

no more concrete cause to which they may assign this disaster than 'the iniquity of the times.' So Oxford had a professor of ancient history and Cambridge had none. Cambridge, however, had for a while 'a reader of the Saxon language and of the history of our ancient British churches': two branches of learning which since Parker's day had been united. The reader was Abraham Wheelock: he also professed Arabic but edited ancient English laws. As reader of Saxon he was paid by Henry Spelman, upon whose death in troublous days (1641) the endowment lapsed. Opportunities had been lost. The age of fresh and vigorous research went by. Cambridge should have had an historical professorship recalling the name of Parker. A line of professors that began with G. J. Vossius would have begun famously.

A decline of interest, or at least of academic interest, in history may be traced by anyone who with a list of the Camden professors before him seeks for their names in that Dictionary of National Biography which is among the best historical products of our own time. During the seventeenth century the Camden professors were men who in some way or another left a mark behind them. Degory Wheare, for example, the first of them, wrote a book on The Method and Order of Reading Histories: a book that can still be read and such a book as a professor should sometimes write. Lewis Dumoulin was a remarkable member of a remarkable family. 'Dodwell's learning was immense,' said Gibbon. Then, however, there was a fall. Thomas Hearne, the under librarian at Oxford, who was a truly zealous student, might, so he said, have filled the chair if he would have bowed the knee to an usurping dynasty. Apparently learning and loyalty were not to be found in combination. Late in the eighteenth century occurs the name of William Scott, who as Lord Stowell was to expound law for the nations. His lectures were well attended (so we are told) and were praised by those whose praise was worth having. His name is followed by that of Thomas Warton, who had already been professor of poetry. His title to the one chair and to the other is not to be disputed, at all events if history is to include the history of literature ; and the versatile man wrote a history of the parish of Kiddington as 'a specimen of a history of Oxfordshire.' But we need trace no further the fortunes of ancient history. It might be considered as a branch of 'the classics' or of 'humane letters,' and the study of it, though flagging, was likely to revive.

We must turn to speak of a royal benefactor. George I, the king, whose title to the crown of Great Britain the learned Hearne would not acknowledge, had 'observed that no encouragement or provision had been made in either of the universities for the study of modern history or modern languages.' Also he had 'seriously weighed the prejudice that had accrued to the said universities from this defect, persons of foreign nations being often employed in the education and tuition of youth both at home and in their travels.' It may well have struck His Majesty that, if it was a defect on his part to speak no English, it was a defect on the part of his ministers to speak no German. Also it may have struck him that a knowledge 'rerum Brunsvicensium,' and, to speak more generally, a knowledge of the Germanic Body and its none too simple history was not so common in England as it might reasonably be expected to be in all parts of His Majesty's dominions. Also it is not impossible that a prince of that house which had Leibnitz for its historiographer may have thought that such historiographers as England could shew hardly reached a creditable standard. So he founded professorships of modern history at Oxford and Cambridge (1724). Out of the stipends that were assigned to them the professors were to provide teachers of the modern languages.

The university of Cambridge, if it wanted learning was not deficient in loyalty, and effusively thanked the occupier of the throne for his 'noble design,' his 'princely intentions.' The masters and scholars 'ventured...to join in the complaint that foreign tutors had so large a share in the education of our youth of quality both at home and in their travels.' They even dared to foresee a glad day when 'there should be a sufficient number of academical persons well versed in the knowledge of foreign courts and well instructed in their respective languages; when a familiarity with the living tongues should be superadded to that of the dead ones; when the solid learning of antiquity should be adorned and set off with a skilful habit of conversing in the languages that now flourish and both be accompanied with English probity; when our nobility and gentry would be under no temptation of sending for persons from foreign countries to be entrusted with the education of their children; and when the appearance of an English gentleman in the courts of Europe with a governor of his own nation would not be so rare and uncommon as it theretofore had been.'

Such were the phrases with which these representatives of English learning welcomed the royal gift. This we know; for if the university of Cambridge was slow to produce a school of history, the borough of Cambridge once had for its town clerk a compiler of admirable annals. The foreigner, we observe, was to be driven from the educational market, and the English gentleman was to appear in foreign courts with a 'governor' of his own nation: in other words the professor of modern history was to be the trainer of bear-leaders: the English leaders of English bears. This being the ideal, it is not perhaps surprising that the man who at that time was doing the best work that was being done in England as a systematic narrator of very modern history was the Frenchman Abel Boyer, or that he should have belonged to the hateful race of foreign tutors. The remoter history of England might be read in the pages of M. de Rapin, or, if 'familiarity with the living tongues' would not extend so far, then in the translation which Mr Tindal was about to publish. In academic eyes modern history was to be an ornamental fringe around 'the solid learning of antiquity.' As to the wretched middle ages, they, it was well understood, had been turned over to 'men of a low, unpolite genius fit only for the rough and barbarick part of learning.' One of these mere antiquaries had lately written a History of the Exchequer which has worn better than most books of its time. Also he had written this sentence: 'In truth, writing of history is in some sort a religious act.' But the spirit which animated Thomas Madox was not at home in academic circles.

It may be that some of the regius professors ably performed the useful task with which they were entrusted. Statistics which should exhibit the nationality of the tutors who made the grand tour with young persons of quality would be hard to obtain, and no unfavourable inference should be drawn from the bare fact that the professor's mastery of history was seldom attested by any book that bore his name. Of one we may read that he is the anonymous author of 'The Country Parson's Advice to his Parishioners of the Younger Sort'; of another that 'he was killed by a fall from his horse when returning...from a dinner with Lord Sandwich at Hinchinbroke.' Macaulay has said that the author of the Elegy in a Country Churchyard was in many respects better qualified for the professorship than any man living. That may be so; but 'the habits of the time made lecturing unnecessary' (so Mr Leslie Stephen has told us), and as a teacher of modern history Thomas Gray must be for us a mute, inglorious potentiality. Historical work was being done even at Cambridge. David Wilkins published the collection of English Concilia which still holds the field and edited the Anglo-Saxon laws; but he, like Wheelock, was professor of Arabic; also he was a German and his name was not Wilkins. To find a square hole for the round man was apparently the fashion of the time. Conyers Middleton professed geology.

If Gibbon learnt much at Oxford he was ungrateful, and yet he was the only member of the historical 'triumvirate' in whom an English university could claim anything. Modern history was at length earning academic honour north of the Tweed when Robertson reigned at Edinburgh. Hume found that history was more profitable than philosophy and consumed less time. His rival in the historical field could in the interval between Peregrine Pickle and Humphrey Clinker turn out history at the rate of a century a month; but he was another beggarly Scot. The demand for history was increasing; the notion of history was extending its bounds. Burke began a history of the laws of England and should have written more than ten pages. Anderson, another Scot, had compiled a solid history of British commerce. Dr Coxe of the House of Austria showed that the travelling tutor might become an industrious and agreeable historian.

About the beginning of the nineteenth century it became usual to appoint to the chairs of modern history men who would take their duties seriously and who either had written or might be expected to write history of one sort or another. Thus Prof. William Smyth, of Cambridge, published lectures that were admired, and Prof. Nares, of Oxford, wrote about Lord Burleigh a book, which as Macaulay's readers will remember, weighed sixty pounds avoirdupois. Thomas Arnold's name occurs in the Oxford list, and, besides all else that he did, he introduced the teaching of modern history into a public school. Nevertheless if we look back at the books that were being produced during the first half of the century, we must confess that a remarkably large amount of historical literature was coming from men who had not been educated at Oxford or Cambridge. One and the same college might indeed boast of Macaulay, Hallam, Thirlwall and Kemble. On the other side stand such names as those of James Mill, Grote, Palgrave, Lingard, Carlyle, Buckle, Napier; and we must not forget Sir Archibald Alison and Sharon Turner; still less such archivists as Petrie and the two Hardys. We cannot say that any organized academic opinion demanded the work that was done by the Record Commission, by the Rolls Series, or by the Historical Manuscripts Commission, or that the universities cried aloud for the publication of State papers and the opening of the national archives. But some Niebuhr was translated and then some Ranke, and it became plain that the sphere of history was expanding in all directions.

Then the great change came, soon after the middle of the century. The professors at the two universities were among the first men that would have been mentioned by anyone who was asked to give the names of our living historians. An opportunity of teaching, and of teaching seriously was being provided for them. Gradually the study of history became the avenue to an 'honours degree.' It was not among the first of 'the new studies' that obtained recognition at Cambridge. The moral sciences and the natural sciences took precedence of it. For a while the moral sciences included a little history (1851). Then (1858), a small place was found for it in the Law Tripos. Then for a few years there was a Law and History Tripos (1870) in which, however, law was the predominant partner. The dissolution of partnership took effect in 1875. History was emancipated. A similar change had been made at Oxford some few years earlier (1872). At Oxford the class list of the school of Modern History has now become nearly if not quite the longest of the class lists. In

Cambridge the competition of the natural sciences has been severer, but the Historical Tripos attracts a number of candidates that is no longer small, and increases. Some new professorships have been founded. Oxford has two chairs of modern, one of ancient, one of ecclesiastical history, besides readerships and lectureships. Cambridge has had a professor of ecclesiastical history since 1884, a professor of ancient history since 1898. Whewell, the historian of inductive science, provided ample encouragement for the study of international law, which is closely related to modern history. Scholarships in 'history, and more especially ecclesiastical history,' were endowed by Lightfoot, the historian of early Christianity. The establishment of prizes for historical essays began at Oxford in the middle of the century when the name of Thomas Arnold was thus commemorated. Other prizes came from Lord Stanhope, who in various ways deserved well of history, and from Lord Lothian. At this point also Cambridge was somewhat behindhand; but the names of the Prince Consort, Thirlwall, and Seeley are now connected with prizes. A list of successful essays shows that in not a few cases the offer of an honourable reward has turned a young man's thoughts to a field in which he has afterwards done excellent work. It is a cause for rejoicing that among the teachers of history at the universities there have been men so justly famous, each in his own way, as Stubbs, Freeman, Froude, Creighton, Hatch, and Seeley—for we will name none but the departed—but when all men get their due a large share of credit will be given to those whose patient and self-denying labours as tutors and lecturers have left them little time for the acquisition of such fame as may be won by great books.

It is, then, of a modern movement and of young schools that these essays speak to us : of a movement which is yet in progress : of schools that have hardly outlived that tentative and experimental stage through which all institutions ought to pass. We may wish for these schools not only the vigour but also the adaptability of youth. And, if it be true, as will be said by others, that there are many reasons why history should be taught, let it not be forgotten that, whether we like it or no, history will be written. The number of men in England who at the present time are writing history of some sort or another must indeed be very large. Very small may be the number of those who take the universe or universal mankind for their theme. Few will be those who aspire so high as the whole life of some one nation. But many a man is writing the history of his county, his parish, his college, his regiment, is endeavouring to tell the tale of some religious doctrine, some form of art or literature, some economic relationship, or some rule of law. Or, again, he is writing a life, or he is editing letters. Nor must we forget the journalists and the history, good, bad, and indifferent that finds a place in their articles; nor the reviewers of historical books, who assume to judge and therefore ought to know.

All this is important work. It has to be done, and will be done, and it ought to be done well, conscientiously, circumspectly, methodically. Now it may be that no school of history can be sure of producing great historians; and it may be that when the great historian appears he will perchance come out of a school of classics or mathematics, or will have given some years to metaphysics or to physiology. But even for his sake we should wish that all the departmental work, if such we may call it, should be thoroughly well performed. His time should not be wasted over bad texts, ill-arranged material, or assertions for which no warrantor is vouched. To help and at any rate not to hinder him should be the hope of many humble labourers.

That is not all. The huge mass of historical stuff that is

now-a-days flowing from the press goes to make the minds of its writers and of its readers, and indeed to make the mind of the nation. It is of some moment that mankind should believe what is true, and disbelieve what is false.

To make Gibbons or Macaulays may be impossible: but it cannot be beyond the power of able teachers to set in the right path many of those who, say what we will, are going to write history well or are going to write it ill. Unquestionably of late years an improvement has taken place in England; but still it is not altogether pleasant to compare English books of what we will again call departmental or sectional history with the parallel books that come to us from abroad. When the *English Historical Review* was started in 1886—at J. R. Green's suggestion, so Creighton has told us—England in one important respect stood behind some small and some backward countries. ' English historians had not yet...associated themselves in the establishment of any academy or other organisation, nor founded any journal to promote their common object.' Even of late Dr Gross has been sending us our bibliographies from the other side of the Atlantic. More co-operation, more organisation, more and better criticism, more advice for beginners are needed. And the need if not met will increase. History is lengthening and widening and deepening. It is lengthening at both ends, for while modern states in many parts of the globe are making new history at a bewilderingly rapid rate, what used to be called ancient history is no longer by any means the ancientest: Egypt, Assyria, Babylonia, and even primeval man are upon our hands. And history is widening. Could we neglect India, China and Japan, there would still be America, Australia, Africa, as well as Europe, demanding that their stories should be told and finding men to tell them well or to tell them badly. And history is deepening. We could not if we would be satisfied with the battles and the protocols, the alliances and the intrigues.   Literature and art, religion and law, rents and prices, creeds and superstitions have burst the political barrier and are no longer to be expelled.   The study of interactions and interdependences is but just beginning, and no one can foresee the end.   There is much to be done by schools of history ; there will be more to be done every year.

THE TEACHING OF
ECCLESIASTICAL HISTORY.

HE that will be a teacher of Ecclesiastical History must lay
it to heart that there is neither art nor mystery in the matter
beyond the art and mystery of teaching History in general.
Ecclesiastical History is not an enchanted ground where the
laws of evidence and common sense are left behind, and
partizanship may run riot without blame. It is simply a
department of General History like Political or Social or
Economic History, and differs no more from these and others
than they do from each other. Each of them leans on the
rest, and in its turn throws light on others. The problems of
one are often the answers of another. They all deal with the
same mass of material, for there is meaning for them all in
every single fact which has ever influenced the development of
men in political or other societies : and they all deal with it in
the same way, obtaining their facts by the same methods of
research, and sifting them by the same principles of criticism.
So far they are unreservedly alike ; for the power of life divine
which works in Ecclesiastical History works equally in the
rest, and works in all by natural laws. The difference is only
that each has a different thread to disentangle from the great
coil. Thus facts which are principal to one are often minor
matters to another. Yet be it noted that it is never safe
entirely to ignore the smallest fact, for History in all its length

and all its breadth is one organic whole, and every single fact of the entire collection has a bearing of some sort on every other.

Our chief aims in the practical teaching of History are three—to rouse interest, to give the guiding facts, and to teach the principles of research and criticism which enable men not only to become their own teachers, but to return and see for themselves how far we rightly gave them the guiding facts. And these three aims are in their natural order. In the case of children, we seek chiefly to rouse their interest, though we give them the simpler guiding facts, and tell them in simple cases where we get them and how we sift them. Our teaching must look forward from the first, and lay foundations for the future. A little further on, the stress falls chiefly on the guiding facts, though neither of the other aims can be neglected. At a third stage, even the ripest of our scholars will thank us for keeping up their interest and giving them fresh guiding facts, though our chief endeavour will be to teach them the methods of criticism and research. The most advanced teaching must always lean on and look back to the elementary things; and these must always stand out clearly from the rest, and be emphasized so far as may be needed to prevent our scholars from losing themselves in a maze of detail.

The teacher must therefore keep all these three aims always more or less in view. The characteristic difference between elementary and advanced teaching is not in the amount of detail, but in the relative prominence of these different aims. Advanced teaching need not always be detailed teaching. It may very well be a mere summary of the teacher's own results, which the students are to test by working out the details for themselves under his general guidance. Just as the teacher who has not learning enough spoils his outline by his imperfect grasp of the details underlying it, so the teacher who has more learning than he can manage thinks it enough to pile up details without bringing out clearly the important points. The one mistake is about as bad as the other; and it is quite possible to commit both at once.

The two chief methods of teaching are by lectures and by papers. Each has its own advantages. Lectures are (or ought to be) fresher and more interesting, and the best means of opening out new ideas; while papers are better suited to follow them up (not at once, but after an interval) and to test and strengthen the student's grasp of his work. Thus (as we shall see more fully later on) the two methods call for somewhat different faculties in the teacher, so that while both methods ought to be used, the individual teacher may fairly lean a little to that for which he feels best qualified. Within certain limits, the work he can do best is the best work he can do for his pupils.

The first thing to be done in lecturing is to get a clear plan for the lecture. This plan may vary greatly from lecture to lecture; but it should always be carefully chosen. It must be simple, and it ought to give a natural arrangement of the matter in hand. Thus the political history of Western Europe for some time after the treaty of Utrecht may be gathered round the efforts of Spain to recover her lost possessions in Italy; and the physical geography of Spain herself will map out well her eight hundred years of conflict with the Moors. But whatever the plan may be, it must be strictly carried out. Digressions are useful enough, and may even form the chief part of the lecture. But any serious digression ought to be planned out beforehand, and all digression must be kept firmly subject to the peremptory condition that there never be a moment's doubt where the thread of the plan is left, and where it is taken up again.

The arrangement of the lecture needs care. The heads should stand out boldly, and there should not be too many of them. If more than five seem wanted, let some of them be grouped together. Even the subdivisions must be clear, and clearly distinguished from the larger headings. If only the arrangement is quite clear, it is none the worse for being a little formal. The wording, on the other hand, should be elastic. Critical sentences will need careful study; but in general, the more freely we speak the better. Half the battle is to watch the class and keep in touch with it, and catch the inspirations of the moment without digressing at random.

The delivery should be slow, so that students may be able to take down most of what is said; and an occasional pause (not merely after a critical sentence) will be a help. If the voice is quickened, it should be an understood sign that students are for the moment to take nothing down. Bad lectures are more commonly made bad by quick speaking, want of pauses, and consequent overpress of details than by faulty arrangement. The young and zealous teacher goes too quickly, doing work for his class which they ought to do for themselves, and crowding his lectures with details better learned from books. The old lecturer who knows his ground and has forgotten his own early difficulties also goes too quickly, throwing down valuable hints for his best men, and leaving the rest to find their way as they can. I have heard of lectures where every word was gold-dust, which yet were largely thrown away, because nobody could take good notes of them. Near akin to quick speaking is another disorderly habit. A lecturer ought not commonly to need a wheelbarrow for his books: and it is a bad sign if he goes home laden like a beast of burden.

How about notes for the lecturer's own use? Some speak without notes; and this is an excellent plan, but only for those who are perfectly sure of themselves. The risk is very great of forgetting parts of the plan, of breaking down in trying to frame critical sentences, or of being tempted into imprudent digressions. Others write out everything, and simply read their notes; and this is commonly fatal. The more our eyes are on the class and the less on notes the better. Lectures must be spoken, not read: and the power to read a manuscript as if it were freshly spoken is one of hard attainment. In its absence, nothing but rare excellence can keep a read lecture from becoming a soporific. The best way is to take in notes full enough to remind us of our plan and help us through any sentences that have to be worded with special care, but not full enough to tempt us into the fatal error of reading them. If these notes are carefully drawn they may with advantage be laid on the table for inspection as soon as the lecture is over. The younger students in particular will learn method from them in the most effective way.

This then seems to be the ideal of a lecture :—plan clear and thoughtful, arrangement clear and rather formal, delivery clear and slow, wording clear and free, but suggestive and precise. Tell your class that every phrase and every turn of a phrase is there for a purpose ; and invite them to take it to pieces, and see with their own eyes and not with yours that things are well and truly stated. I am satisfied that a lecture which fairly aims at this ideal will be almost equally useful to students who differ widely in attainment. The weakest absolutely need the clear plan of the lecture to guide their reading, and will get strong encouragement from every glimpse of its deeper meaning ; while even the strongest are always glad of a clean suggestive outline, full of hints for further study.

Some will think this ideal pitched too high, at least for the Poll man. I have not found it so. Give him your best, and take extra pains to make sure that everything is quite clear ; but do not lecture down to him. He will often answer splendidly, if he is properly appealed to. Your conversation class at the end of the term will be a pelt of eager questions ; and long before the year is out you will see waves pass through the room like the wind over the corn—sometimes even the lecturer's crowning triumph, when every pen drops of itself in close and eager listening, as if a signal had been given. The teacher can commit no more crying sin than in thinking that inferior work is good enough for backward students. Said a former College tutor to me once, "You know you cannot do much with the Poll man. I find it as much as he can manage if I give him a few simple questions, and expect an answer in the words of the book." He was not famed for success in teaching the Poll man.

We pass now from lectures to papers. Both are commonly needed. Lectures are likely to evaporate if they are not followed up by papers ; and papers are likely to be fragmentary work if no foundation has been laid for them by lectures. Fifteen or twenty years ago papers were very commonly looked on as menial work, but I hope that idea is nearly dead now. In truth, the task of looking over a paper thoroughly is very much harder than that of giving a good lecture. It is not enough to score the answers overnight, and in the morning deliver a general harangue on all things and certain other things. Another plan is to look over the paper with each man singly, thereby securing him the overestimated "benefit of individual attention." But if this is not done perfunctorily it consumes an enormous amount of time ; and (what is worse) it throws away the important help which students can be made to give each other. There is a better way than this, but a much harder one.

In my later years of private teaching the excessive number of lectures to which theological students were driven (often two, three, or even four in a morning) compelled me to do most of my work by papers. The plan finally hammered out was this. The class was six or seven. A smaller number did not give enough variety, and a much larger one was unwieldy. As variety was an object no care was taken to sort the men. Strong and weak sat in the same class, and with the best results. The weak sometimes helped and seldom hindered the strong, while the strong helped the weak enormously. There were three, four, at utmost five questions in the paper, with perhaps three or four more below a line. These last were quite optional, and seldom answered ; but a few words at the end were enough to shew the way of dealing with them. The questions, especially those above the line, were big subjects, more or less of an essay character, which required a fair amount of reading and considerable grasp of mind to do them really well. Easy questions were avoided. If anyone could not do the whole paper he had standing orders to bring two answers done in outline rather than one completely: yet if anyone pleased he was welcome every now and then to throw his entire strength on a single question, doing it much more thoroughly than usual. Then I took the first man's answer to the first question, and commented on it there and then, not only for his own benefit, but for the class; and so on round the table, summing up myself at the end, and perhaps giving my own answer. After this the next question, beginning with another man. This is a plan which draws heavily on the teacher. In lecturing he has only to put the subject in the best way he can find: but here he must take it up at a moment's notice by any handle that may be offered him. He must see through the whole structure of the answer at a glance, and recognize in a moment the whole process by which it was put together. Then comes the criticism; and this will task to the uttermost his command of the subject. Mere slips of grammar or fact he scores quietly: but these are small matters. Sometimes he reads out an extract from an answer, sometimes he outlines it for public benefit, sometimes he tells two men to read each other's papers (rather a stretch of authority), sometimes he invites the class to dissect some tempting half truth, sometimes he calls attention to some new view of the matter, and occasionally he puts in a quiet hit at some bit of petty naughtiness at the far end of the table. Misbehaviour of any consequence I met with less than half-a-dozen times in more than twenty years.

The first advantage of this plan is that each man not only does the question himself but gets the salient points of half-a-dozen other men's answers picked out for him and discussed before the teacher sums up himself. True, the weaker men find the questions very hard, and often wholly miss the point of them. But they soon begin to see that if they have honestly done what they can, they always know enough about the matter to see its bearings when they are pointed out in class : and meanwhile their occasional successes and even half successes will give them courage. A man gains new confidence when for the first time he has done a hard question better than some to whom he has always looked up. But here the teacher needs all his gentleness. Let him above all things beware of impatiently brushing aside an imperfect answer as worthless. He must give the man credit for every touch of insight, and even for honest work that has turned out a failure, and then take it just as it stands, and gently lay open the misconception which has done the mischief. A very little roughness or want of sympathy will utterly ruin this part of the work.

Another advantage is that men are drawn together, and the class becomes more or less a society for friendly study. It represents a German *Seminar* on a lower plane. Men not only have abundant samples of method, but get used to hearing subjects of their own reading discussed from all points of view. The beginner cannot do much more than get up what he finds in his book ; and from this point we must lead him on to look all round things, to see their connexions, to use his own judgment, and to recognize old problems under all disguises. Whatever questions may come before him in the Tripos he must know exactly the method of dealing with them. The flexibility of mind required to do this is even more distinctive of the educated man than his learning ; and I know no better training for it than by such papers as are here described.

Lectures and papers must be the staple of our regular teaching. Essays may have to be prepared for ; but students who are well trained on papers will not need to devote any very great attention to them. On the other hand, the conversation class is an occasional help of great importance. In this the Socratic method is a powerful weapon in skilled and gentle hands, especially for clearing up elementary ideas ; but

I have never felt myself quite equal to it. I therefore did the clearing chiefly in the papers, and devoted the conversation class to humbler uses. The men were told to look up difficulties, bring their note-books, and ask what they liked. They generally managed a good bombardment of questions. There was no great harm if the talking was chiefly done by a few of the best men ; for if their questions were not quite representative, they were all the more useful and suggestive. They generally got quite as much from a conversation class as from a lecture. Nor is the teacher who simply stands and answers questions quite so passive as he seems. If he wants a particular question asked, he can generally force it as a conjuror forces a card, by properly shaping his answers. He can be active enough if he pleases.

Guidance rather than teaching is needed by students of a riper sort, who are ready or nearly ready for original research. In Cambridge either the Theological or the Historical Tripos will now give an excellent training in historical method. A man who goes through either, and takes a good place in his Second Part, has laid a broad foundation for future work, and made a good start with the critical study and comparison of original writers. When a man has once reached this point, historical teaching proper falls into the background, though he may still want special help from the philosopher, the antiquarian, the palæographer, the economist, or the teacher of languages. The German *Seminar* is in itself excellent : but it has never taken root in Cambridge. Only a few students yearly are equal to the work, and most of these either go down as soon as they have taken their degree, or if they stay in residence they are most likely reading for some other Tripos or competing for some University distinction, or possibly already preparing a dissertation, so that hardly any have leisure to join a *Seminar*. When a man is ready to undertake a dissertation, the only help that can be given him is some general information about books and original authorities, and perhaps a few general cautions about wider aspects of the subject which he may be in danger of overlooking.

As regards the teaching of Ecclesiastical as distinct from that of General History, I really have nothing to say. I will not even put in a caution against the *odium theologicum*, for this is no special disease of Theology, but the common pest of all studies. Quarrelsome dogs can always get up a fight; and bone for bone of contention, bimetallism is as good as transubstantiation. I hear say that artists can disagree; and I have seen a very pretty quarrel over the Gulf Stream. The only difference is that ecclesiastical language has a few peculiarities.

THE TEACHING OF PALAEOGRAPHY
AND DIPLOMATIC.

THE name Diplomatic is traced back to the illustrious
Jean Mabillon, who in his treatise *De Re Diplomatica*, first
published in 1681, laid the foundations of the science. The
tradition which he left among his brethren of the Congregation
of St Maur was loyally maintained by them; and it is to two of
his successors, Dom Toustain and Dom Tassin, that we owe
the second great treatise on the subject, the *Nouveau Traité de
Diplomatique*, which appeared in six volumes between 1750
and 1765. Here we have *Diplomatique* as a substantive, and
hence the word found its way into Germany, Italy, and
England; though the modern Germans prefer to use their own
word *Urkundenlehre*. Diplomatic, according to its etymology,
is the science of *documents*, but Mabillon used the word in a
broader sense, to include everything connected with the rules
of *writing* as well. It was only by degrees that these rules
were differentiated to form a separate science of Palaeography.
The distinction may be put in this way: Diplomatic has
nothing to do with writing in itself; Palaeography has to do
exclusively with writing. Or again, Palaeography deals with
the external elements of a written text; Diplomatic, with its
internal organism. The palaeographer studies the forms of
written characters, the history of the alphabet, and of the
styles of writing used in different countries and in different

ages. He examines the materials on which writing is found, analyses the ink in which it is written, describes the miniatures with which a book is decorated. But it is not his part to interpret what is written : his function is to explain the outer form. Palaeography thus is concerned with a far wider field than Diplomatic ; it takes in all written books and documents in all languages and of all ages : but it does not go behind the writing. Diplomatic on the other hand is limited to documents, and practically to the forms and styles of documents which grew up under the later Roman Empire and among the barbarian invaders, in a system which has continued, though with manifold changes, down to our own day. The two studies thus distinguished have a certain margin of common territory ; and if a palaeographer in many departments of his work can afford to dispense with Diplomatic, the diplomatist cannot proceed far without a knowledge of Palaeography. Both studies are limited, in different ways, to the form of a written text, and are thus excluded from the province of the historian, since he is occupied with its matter. Yet the historian has need of Diplomatic, as the primarily critical science, to enable him to discern between the genuine and the spurious, and the diplomatist on his side must consult the historian in order to obtain working data for many of the principles he has to establish.

With Palaeography we are only here concerned in so far as it is connected with Diplomatic and History. Practically we are limited to Medieval Latin Palaeography, for the broken-down types of handwriting which followed the invention of printing are too irregular to be brought under any scientific definition, and the technical court-hand of our lawyers is a professional development—or rather an artificial perversion—of a known style, by the help of which it can be mastered with a little practice. Classical Palaeography, on which courses of lectures are frequently given by the Professors of Greek and Latin at Oxford, and for which there is a special Readership at

Cambridge, lies in itself outside our range. But the lessons of Classical Palaeography, with which we may include that of Biblical manuscripts, are themselves of abundant value for the historical student, since they furnish him with the best equipment for the textual criticism of his authorities. For the copyist of historical works was liable to the same errors as one who transcribed other books, and the sources and modes of textual corruption have been the subjects of the most complete examination in connexion with Biblical and Classical writings.

At Oxford there has been established for many years past a Lectureship in Medieval Palaeography which its learned holder, Mr Falconer Madan, has sought to make serviceable 'for persons studying for the Classical or Modern History Schools.' We may take his method as a model for such teaching. Unfortunately the arrangement made by the University provides only for one course of lectures in each year. While therefore Mr Madan drew out his lectures on a scheme extending over three years, he had to take into consideration the certainty that some members of his class each year would be beginners. Accordingly he devised the ingenious expedient of sometimes breaking up his course of lectures delivered twice a week into two separate courses; so that, for instance, the Tuesday lectures might form the continuation of the previous year's course, while the Thursday lectures, or a part of them, might form an elementary course for beginners. A full syllabus was printed so that students might know what was new and what old. Mr Madan by degrees greatly increased the usefulness of his teaching by the provision of thirty-six facsimiles of manuscripts, which are circulated among the class or can be purchased if desired. And thus as the collection of facsimiles was made more complete and representative, it became possible to economise time in the explanation of details, and to combine a permanent introductory course with a varying element of more advanced instruction. It will be well to illustrate the system both of the double and single lectures by giving the main points in Mr Madan's syllabus for two different years, 1891 and 1897. In the latter the references to the facsimiles, which occupy a prominent place in the original, have been omitted.

I.

1. The scope and use of Palaeography.
2. The history of the Alphabet.
    3. The Genealogy of Western Handwritings.
4. Abbreviations and Contractions.
    5. Handwritings of the British Isles to A.D. 900.
6. Forms of Letters A—E.
    7. The Caroline Minuscule in the ninth and tenth centuries.
8. Letters F—M.
    9. The eleventh century, especially in England.
10. Letters N—R.
    11. Book Production in the Middle Ages.
12. Letters S—Z, Numerals, &c.
    13. The application of Palaeography to Textual Criticism.
14. Informal (how to collate and describe MSS.).

II.

1. The Alphabet.
2. Writing in Western Europe to A.D. 800.
3. Early writing in the British Isles.
4. Contractions.
5. The Continental hand in the 10th and 11th centuries.
6. The extinction of English national writing.
7. The 12th century.
8. The change to a Gothic hand.
9. Court-hand of the 13th century.
10. The 14th century.

The student of Palaeography has the advantage of an admirable textbook in English in Sir Edward Maunde Thompson's *Greek and Latin Palaeography* (2nd edition, 1894). In French we may mention two treatises, the *Manuel de Paléographie* by M. Prou (1890), and *Éléments de Paléographie* by Canon Reusens (1899). It is to be regretted that no treatise exists on the special Palaeography of English manuscripts. Sir Edward Thompson's book is furnished with a good selection of facsimiles. Most of these however are necessarily reduced in size, and it is desirable to have constant recourse to the large specimens which have been reproduced by the autotype process in five great volumes by the Palaeographical Society. Similar collections, though none on so comprehensive a scale, have been published in France, Germany, and Italy ; but the volumes of the Palaeographical Society are the most accessible in England. Two small collections may also be mentioned, which, though published primarily with a literary object, will be found useful by persons working at the development of medieval handwriting for the purposes of historical study. These are Professor R. Ellis's *Facsimiles from Latin MSS. in the Bodleian Library* and Professor Skeat's *Twelve Facsimiles of Old English Manuscripts.* The study of the subject must necessarily be carried on with the help of facsimiles at every stage ; and these can now be produced so cheaply that every teacher can if he pleases form a small collection of his own in a sufficient number of copies to serve for study in a class. If he has these transferred to lantern slides he will gain a great advantage in pointing out minute details on the screen ; but lectures delivered in a darkened room have drawbacks to those who wish to take notes.

It is of the first importance to learn not only how to read a manuscript but also how to assign its date. The two acquirements indeed are closely related; for the reason why one reads a particular letter in a particular way is that it belongs to a particular time. The same sign means *w* in the Anglo Saxon of the tenth century, and *y* in the English of the thirteenth; the *r* of one age is hardly to be distinguished from the *n* of another; and so forth. But the beginner must never be misled into believing—what is sometimes maintained by persons who ought to know better—that a single letter will serve to date a manuscript, or that there is any absolute point of time before or after which a given form is impossible. He must learn to judge the age of a manuscript by the general type and character which it presents, and then test his conclusion by examining the letters in detail. But he must never forget that handwriting like architecture changed imperceptibly, under various influences and at various places. Allowance must also be made for the age of the individual scribe, which is seldom known; since an elderly man will usually preserve the style of writing in which he was brought up. With practice the student will be able to mark the peculiarities of different countries. He will even discern the features of a particular *scriptorium*, as that of St Martin's at Tours in Carolingian times, of St Paul's Cathedral in the twelfth century, or of St Alban's Abbey in the thirteenth. When we come to manuscripts in modern languages, a knowledge of the history of phonetic changes and of dialects helps us to assign date and place; and the Humanist movement remodels the spelling of Latin. But considerations such as these last are secondary. They must not be applied by themselves to fix the date of a manuscript, but only to corroborate a result arrived at on properly palaeographical grounds.

Recent discoveries of papyri have added very largely to the materials for study, specially for that of the ancient Greek and Roman cursive hands. But if we are learning Palaeography

with the view of working at the sources of medieval history, we
can leave this very intricate department of the subject almost
altogether on one side.   It will indeed help us to understand the
origines of the National hands, as they are called,—distinguished
by the misleading names, Visigothic, Merovingian, and Lom-
bardic;—but hardly to interpret them.   Indeed the modern
historian only comes directly into contact with the Roman
cursive if he has occasion to study the documents of the Exar-
chate, and their interest is to a larger extent diplomatic than
palaeographical.   For general purposes of study it is sufficient
to begin with the Uncial type, the Irish and English hands,
the National hands, the Half-Uncial, and the Caroline
Minuscule, the formed Book-hand of the later middle ages, and
the Court-hand of charters.   If our object is antiquarian, to deal
with English local or family records, it is not a bad plan to
begin with the beautifully clear writing which we find in the
charters of the reign of King John, and to work downwards
until in the fifteenth century on the one hand it breaks down
altogether, and on the other crystallises into the highly technical
forms of the modern Court and Chancery hands.

For the learning of abbreviations a dictionary of some
sort is essential.   The great *Lexicon Diplomaticum* of Walther
(1756) is still the most extensive work of reference.   Smaller
works are those of A. Chassant (5th edition, 1884), C. Trice
Martin (*The Record Interpreter*, 1892, an enlargement of the
appendix to his edition of Wright's *Court Hand Restored*), and
A. Cappelli (*Dizionario dei Abbreviature*, 1899).   There is
also a dictionary of abbreviations given by Sir Thomas Duffus
Hardy in the *Registrum Sacrum Palatinum*, vol. iii., which is
serviceable for English manuscripts.

It has seemed sufficient to give a bare suggestion of hints
and cautions, because the student of Palaeography is supplied
with the necessary textbooks.   In Diplomatic it is otherwise.
The Englishman who wishes to learn the subject is totally
without any methodical guide.   He may read its general prin-

ciples in the excellent *Manuel de Diplomatique* of the late
M. Giry (1894) or the still more copious but as yet unfinished
Handbuch der Urkundenlehre in Deutschland und Italien of
Professor Bresslau (vol. i., 1889). But only in the former of
these, and there very summarily, will he find anything about the
special documentary forms used in England. Among English
writers George Hickes, the Nonjuring Dean of Worcester, in his
Linguarum Septentrionalium Thesaurus (1703—1705), was the
first to deal at all specially with Anglo-Saxon documents; and
Thomas Madox in the preface to his *Formulare Anglicanum*
(1702) set out very clearly the relation between the terms of
charters and their legal import. But in the two centuries that
have passed since Hickes and Madox little indeed has been published on the subject. Andrew Wright's *Court-Hand Restored*,
first published in 1773 (9th Edition by Mr C. T. Martin, 1879),
was written with a purely practical purpose, as *The Student's
Assistant in reading Old Deeds, Charters, Records, etc.*; but it
may be applied to the study of the development of the forms
of documents as well. We have some remarks, of real value,
though in part uncritical and erroneous, in the preface to
Kemble's *Codex Diplomaticus Aevi Saxonici* (1839–1848),
and others by Sir Thomas Duffus Hardy in the prefaces to
the *Charter, Patent,* and *Close Rolls of King John* (1833–1837).
Professor Earle in his *Handbook to the Land Charters and
other Saxonic Documents* (1888), has improved upon Kemble,
and Professor Maitland, partly with the help of Brunner, has
in a few paragraphs of his *Domesday Book and Beyond* (1897)
shed more light on the origin and meaning of the Anglo-Saxon
diploma than anyone before him. Lastly Professor Napier
and Mr W. H. Stevenson have furnished contributions of
extreme value to the criticism of a small number of documents
contained in the *Crawford Collection* (1895). Nor should
reference be omitted to Mr J. H. Round's many important
detached essays and notes on Norman and Angevin documents,
though these are not strictly diplomatic, since to Mr Round

the form is only of interest in so far as it illustrates the matter.

The teacher of Diplomatic has therefore, so far as England is concerned, to construct his science largely by himself with the help of the original charters still preserved. Happily these, for the Anglo-Saxon period, immensely surpass in number those of any other country for the same time, and most of them have been reproduced in facsimile by the Ordnance Survey and the Trustees of the British Museum. After the Norman Conquest originals exist in great plenty, and the official enrolments of the Exchequer and the Chancery begin respectively under King Henry I. and King John. It is hardly necessary to add that the documents preserved in transcripts of a somewhat or a much later date, are far more numerous than the originals. But the fact that so large a number of originals remains to us is an enormous advantage to the student; for Diplomatic, as we have said, is primarily a critical science, and to establish the rules of criticism with certainty we require originals as a basis. No one can be confident that a transcript has not been tampered with, consciously or unconsciously, in the very points which we need in order to ascertain whether it is genuine or spurious. To take a simple example, suppose that we find a document preserved in a transcript which begins *Henricus rex Anglie* and claims to emanate from the chancery of King Henry I. We know that this king was *rex Anglorum*; the scribe is merely introducing thoughtlessly the later style of the Plantagenets, having probably the abbreviated *Angł* in the original before him. No argument for or against its genuineness can be drawn from the fault in the title. But had the *Anglie* occurred in a professing original, it could be set down at once as a forgery.

It is essential at the outset to define the limits of the science of Diplomatic. It deals, we have said, with documents, but only with documents in a narrow and technical sense. The word *document* is often, and rightly, used to denote anything which the historian may take as evidence. It may include an inscription, a coin, or a chronicle. But none of these is a document in the diplomatic acceptation, which includes only such documents as might be brought as evidence in a court of law; that is to say, charters, rolls, accounts, and the like. It is important to bear in mind the technical limitation of the term Diplomatic, for in consequence of the earlier usage of the word, as including Palaeography, it is common to find the expression 'diplomatic evidence' as a synonym for 'the evidence of manuscripts,' and a 'diplomatic text' for one which strictly reproduces the features of a manuscript. No book, as such, is a document; but many books,— registers, chartularies, and historical works,—contain documents; and when originals fail us, we have to take recourse to such transcripts in later collections. But it is only when we have originals before us that we can be absolutely safe. The details of style, of formulae, of modes of ratification, are apt to be corrupted in transcription; and the forms of one age are silently, even unconsciously, exchanged for those of another. Our primary concern is therefore with originals. We have to trace their forms at different times, in different countries, in different chanceries; and from these to establish the criteria of genuineness. Forgery plays a large part in the production of medieval documents, and it is the business of the diplomatist to lay down rules for sifting out the false from the true.

The study of originals will also save us from a pitfall in which until recent years scholars often stumbled. They assumed the rules of a given chancery to be invariably, inflexibly observed, and when they found any deviations from them they put down the document without further question as spurious or at least as corrupt. This method has been largely superseded through the work of two leading Austrian critics, Professor Julius Ficker and Freiherr von Sickel. The latter elaborated the principle of the comparison of handwriting; and when it is once proved that a number of documents are written in the autograph of the same chancery official, their genuineness is established, no matter what small errors, *e.g.* in dating, they may present. The former explored the development of the single document in its various stages, from the *petition* on which it was founded, the *draught* which embodied the substance of the petition, and the fair copy, to the final attestation and execution of this last, which turned it into what we call the *original.* When we pass from the original to the *transcript* the investigation becomes more complicated. The labours of these scholars have demolished many cut-and-dried theories; but they have at the same time led to a good deal of hypercriticism in the hands of less competent students. If it is argued that a forgery is based upon a genuine original of somewhat different purport and worked up with the help of another document of the same time and chancery, it is clear that we have an opening for hypothetical theories which unless controlled with judgment will end in purely conjectural results. With reference to Sickel's method, it may be added that the comparison of handwriting leads naturally to the comparison of style, and that the study of the technical language (*dictamen*) of certain types of documents has been employed with success for the purposes of criticism.

A debateable territory between the diplomatist and the historian lies in the region of private letters, despatches, and reports. They belong mainly to the historian, and it is only the formal elements which concern the diplomatist. This is the test all through: the historical matter may be of use in helping the establishment of diplomatic principles, but it is not itself diplomatic.

Within the strict and limited class of documents there is a distinction to be insisted upon, which involves a legal as well as a diplomatic interest. One class of documents produces a new state of things; for instance, a certain deed by itself changes the property of a piece of land from A's hand to B's; it is the vehicle of the grant. Another class merely records or notifies a state of things already existing: as when a king makes known to all men in his realm that he has granted a certain piece of land to *C*. Both classes serve as legal proof of the act done; but in the former case the act is not complete until the document is drawn up, in the latter the document has no influence on the disposition, it merely declares the fact that it has been made. The effective document is the *diploma* (or *charta* in the narrow sense); the notifying document is the *notitia* (or *writ*). Either of them may be in the form of a *letter*.

The elements of which a document is composed are necessarily varied according to the purport of the document; they are customarily varied according to the usages of different countries and times; and they are classified variously by almost every writer upon the subject. It does not really matter much how we construct our classification, so long as we understand what we mean by the terms we use, and so long as we remember that not all the component parts are uniformly found, nor always arranged in the same order. It is the business of the teacher of Diplomatic to draw out the differences in detail. Here we can only give a general statement of the normal elements in a document.

A document is a series of formulae built upon a definite system. It consists of two parts. One is the *text*, or body, which contains the substance or legal purport of the document. This is usually placed in the middle, between the two parts of the *protocol*, or more strictly between the *protocol* and the *eschatocol*. These parts are subdivided as follows :

i. PROTOCOL.

    1. The *Invocation* or *Chrism* (from the ΧΡ[ΙΣΤΟΣ] monogram which often takes its place).

    2. The *Title* (*Superscriptio*), giving the name and style of the grantor. This is often accompanied by the *grace* or formula of devotion (*Dei gratia* or the like).

3. The *Address* (*Inscriptio*), giving the name or names of the person or persons to whom the document is directed.

4. The *Greeting* (*Salutatio*).

ii. TEXT.

1. The *Proem* (*Arenga*), stating in general terms the motive for the act effected or declared in the document. This is commonly limited to the expression of religious sentiments, and is herein distinguished from what we call a Preamble, which has more in common with the Narratio.

2. The *Notification* (*Promulgatio*).

3. The *Statement* of the case (*Narratio*).

4. The *Enacting* or *Operative Clause* (*Dispositio*).

5. The *Penal Clause* or *Clauses* (*Sanctio*).

6. The *Notice of Authentication* (*Corroboratio*).

iii. FINAL PROTOCOL or ESCHATOCOL.

1. The *Names* (*Subscriptiones*) or *Marks* (*Signationes*) of witnesses, of the grantor, and of the chancery official or scribe.

2. The *Date of Place*.

3. The *Date of Time*.

4. The *Amen* or similar religious ending (including the *Appreciatio*, a prayer for the effectuating of the deed).

This enumeration is not complete ; but it indicates generally the features which may be expected to appear in a solemn form of diploma. It is important to notice whether the document has any special marks of authentication and what form of seal, if any, it bears. The study of Seals has indeed been specialised as a distinct study—*Sphragistic*;—but it comes most conveniently under the head of Diplomatic.

The mention of the *date* leads us to observe that though

Chronology is of course a science by itself, yet its study is so essential to that of Diplomatic that (in spite of the arguments of certain purists) no course of instruction in this subject is complete which does not include a full treatment of technical Chronology. In History one may go very far without any more extensive knowledge of Chronology than that which concerns the date of the beginning of the year, the difference between Old and New Style, the dates of Easter and of some of the chief Holy Days. In Diplomatic, on the other hand, one can hardly proceed a step without requiring an exact knowledge of the chronological systems which prevailed in the middle ages ; and for this reason, that a large proportion of our documents are dated in an imperfect manner. Some documents indeed bear such scanty notes of date that no knowledge of Chronology by itself will help us. We have to call in the assistance of Palaeography and of History ; and we have known the case of a letter in which these aids have fixed the single indication 'Tuesday' to the definite day, 16 Dec. 1292. More commonly we have to combine the historical data (*e.g.*, the Regnal Years of kings) with those of Chronology; and the more thorough our knowledge of Chronology, the more likely we are to arrive at a certain conclusion in regard to imperfectly dated documents.

The points to be specially borne in mind are (1) the days of the week, (2) the days of the month, (3) Holy Days, (4) the reckoning of years, with particular notice of the various ways of beginning the year.

(1) With respect to the days of the week it is only necessary here to say that when specified in a document in connexion with some other date they often furnish an immediate guide to the required year. For example, if we have a document of the reign of King Henry IV. dated on Friday, the morrow of SS. Peter and Paul, we can fix it immediately to 1402. For Friday, 30 June, requires a Sunday Letter A, and this only occurred during the supposed reign in 1402. As the calendar year begins and ends on the same week-day, every successive

year begins naturally one day later than that preceding it, so that, were it not for leap year, we should find the same week-days recurring on the same days of the month every seven years. The intercalated day in Leap Year[1] disturbs this regularity, so that it is impossible without calculation or a reference to tables to say how often in a given period of time the same week-days will fall on the same days of the month. If one uses tables it should be remembered (as is indeed obvious) that as the week-day goes forwards the Sunday Letter goes backwards. But it is very desirable to commit to memory some ready means of finding in a moment the day of the week for any given year. The simplest, though not the most scientific, method is that of Father Chambeau, S. J., in which one adds together five numbers and divides by seven ; the remainder giving the day of the week, Sunday being 1, Monday 2, and so forth. The five numbers are these :

1. The year in the century.

2. One quarter of this, omitting fractions (to allow for the leap years).

3. The month number.

Jan.	Feb.	Mar.	April.	May.	June.	July.	Aug.	Sept.	Oct.	Nov.	Dec.
1	4	4	0	2	5	0	3	6	1	4	6

These correspond to the Lunar Regulars, and are not hard to remember. In leap year, January and February 1—24 have to be diminished by 1.

4. The day of the month.

5. The style number. In the Julian calendar (Old Style) this is 18 *minus* the number of the century. In the Gregorian calendar (New Style) it is

22 down to 1699
21 from 1700 to 1799
20 „ 1800 „ 1899.

[1] Note that this day is not 29 February but the day before the 6th of the kalends of March, *i.e.* 24 February. Hence St Matthias' Day in leap year was kept on 25 February.

To illustrate this by an example, King John was crowned on 27 May, 1199. We set down

$$
\begin{array}{r}
99 \\
24 \text{ (the quarter)} \\
2 \text{ (the month number)} \\
27 \text{ (the day of the month)} \\
18 - 11 = \underline{7} \text{ (the style number)} \\
\hline
7)\underline{159}
\end{array}
$$

22—remainder 5 = Thursday, and we know it was Ascension Day.

The process may be simplified by casting out sevens at each stage, thus :

$$
\begin{array}{r}
1 \\
3 \\
2 \\
6 \\
\underline{0} \\
\hline
7)\underline{12}
\end{array}
$$

1—remainder 5 = Thursday.

(2) The days of the month were reckoned either after the old Roman method by kalends, nones, and ides, or else in the modern way from the first onwards. But there are peculiar systems, that of Bologna and the *Cisiojanus*, which require to be mastered separately.

(3) Holy Days were very commonly employed, especially in the later middle ages, for the dating of documents. Lists of Saints with their days will be found in M. Giry's *Manuel de Diplomatique* and in all the books on Chronology. It is important to bear in mind that the day on which a saint was venerated was often not the same in all countries ; and that when a saint had more than one day (*e.g.* a Translation as well as a Deposition) it depended upon local usage which day was denoted by the simple name. Movable feasts are among the

most troublesome and at the same time the most serviceable indications for determining dates. Their relations can be calculated from Easter tables; and there is a series of 35 complete calendars for all possible years given by De Morgan and Grotefend.

(4) Years have been reckoned in many ways. The Romans dated by the consuls of the year, and when the consulate coalesced with the Empire by the *post consulatum* of the Emperor, which was nearly the same as a computation by Regnal years. In the fourth century the *Indiction*, a cycle of 15 years, beginning as it seems in 297, came into use. This only tells us the place of a year within a given cycle of 15; it does not tell us which cycle in the series is meant. The *Spanish Era* was a reckoning of years continuously from 38 B.C., which remained in use in the Peninsula until the fourteenth century.

Lastly there was the *Year of our Lord*, which was fixed by Dionysius Exiguus in the sixth century, but was not employed as a means of dating documents until the Venerable Bede in his treatise *De Temporum Ratione* (725) gave it the weight of his authority. It was not however used in the Imperial chancery until the ninth century, nor in the Papal until the tenth. While it gradually superseded all other modes of computation, there was nothing like agreement as to the day on which the year began. The year of the Incarnation might be considered to begin with the Annunciation (25 March) or with the Nativity (25 Dec.); in the one case the beginning of the year was antedated, as compared with modern usage, by more than nine months, in the other by a week. The inconvenience of the former method must have been early felt, and it became usual to reckon the Annunciation from the 25th March following. Thus year 1000 would begin according to the style of Pisa on 25 March, 999, according to the Imperial and Anglo-Saxon reckoning on 25 Dec. 999, and according to the style of Florence on 25 March, 1000. The Venetians again began it on 1 March, and the French style on Easter Day. All these diverse manners of counting years require to be carefully learnt not merely for different periods and countries, but even for different parts of the same country. It might be shewn for instance that the dating the year from Christmas continued at St Alban's long after it had been superseded in the greater part of England by the Florentine style. But enough has been said to illustrate the necessity of the study of Chronology for the purpose of fixing the dates of documents and criticising their genuineness.

The following list of books on Chronology is limited to those which are of moderate compass and which will be found specially serviceable to English students of Diplomatic.

> Sir Harris Nicolas' *Chronology of History* (1833; new ed. 1840).
>
> A. de Morgan's *Book of Almanacs* (1851).
>
> J. J. Bond's *Handy Book of Rules and Tables for verifying Dates* (1875; 4th ed. 1889), ill arranged but useful.
>
> H. Grotefend's *Zeitrechnung des Deutschen Mittelalters und der Neuzeit* (1891–1898), and *Taschenbuch der Zeitrechnung u. s. w.* (1898); both beautifully printed, and the former very comprehensive.
>
> F. Rühl's *Chronologie des Mittelalters und der Neuzeit* (1897), a very instructive little treatise.

But reference cannot be omitted to the classical *Art de vérifier les Dates* (1750; 4th ed. in 44 volumes, 1818–1844), which forms the basis of most modern works—notably of L. de Mas Latrie's *Trésor de Chronologie* (1889)—and to the not less classical treatise of L. Ideler, *Handbuch der mathematischen und technischen Chronologie* (1825–1826). The section on chronology in M. Giry's *Manuel de Diplomatique* is also scholarly and extremely clear.

If Chronology has been discussed at a length greatly out of proportion to the place which it properly occupies in the study of Diplomatic, the writer's excuse must be that it is a subject which lends itself to a general treatment, whereas it would be quite impossible to give even an outline of the subject-matter of Diplomatic within the limits to which this chapter is confined.

The order in which the history of the different chanceries should be studied is one concerning which a great variety of opinion is permissible. It should be remembered that Diplomatic far more than Palaeography has a national connexion. The student of manuscripts can study the types of many countries without leaving England; the student of documents on the other hand will be thrown mainly upon native materials. Hence the order in which the subject is taught should with us be made to lead up to England. A convenient arrangement is to begin with Papal documents, which have the advantage of simplicity in their structure and at the same time of developing the greatest possible regularity of form and diction. Next we may take Frankish documents, ascending to those of the Empire, and handing on a double succession in France and in Germany. Thirdly, the Anglo-Saxon *diploma*, which came straight from middle Italy, may properly be treated, and the varieties in its form discussed, until in the tenth century it encountered a rival—the *writ*—by which it was finally dispossessed. The eleventh century brought in continental influences again, so that both at the beginning and in the middle it is impossible to study English Diplomatic as a subject by itself. To enter further into the development of the different chanceries would take us beyond the limits of the present chapter.

We conclude by stating briefly what provision is made for the teaching of Palaeography and Diplomatic. At Oxford both subjects have been entrusted to University Lecturers. At Cambridge, besides the Readership in Palaeography already mentioned, occasional recognition is given to both studies by means of the Sandars Lectureship. In London, at the London School of Economics and Political Science, regular courses are given chiefly with a practical view to preparing students for work at the Public Record Office and the British Museum. Every German University offers lectures more or less regularly, the larger ones regularly, with more than one Professor or Privatdocent, both on Palaeography and Diplomatic; but nowhere is the entire subject so completely organised as at Paris. At the École des Chartes the course is one of three years. In the first year (we take the syllabus of 1896–7) there are lectures (1) on Palaeography, (2) on Romance Philology, each twice a week, (3) on Bibliography, once a week: in the second, (1) on Diplomatic, (2) on the History of French Institutions, each twice a week, (3) on the Authorities for French History, (4) on the Management of Archives, each once a week: in the third, (1) on the History of Civil and Canon Law, twice a week, (2) on Medieval Archaeology, (3) on the Authorities for French History, each once a week. By the help of this institution France has trained a body of expert palaeographers, diplomatic scholars, and archivists, unsurpassed in any other country. Yet the German and Austrian schools, even though occasionally discredited by the ill-informed excesses of their disciples, still hold the first place for the systematic character of their work and for the technical perfection of their method.

THE TEACHING OF ANCIENT HISTORY.

WHEN we use the term 'History' we commonly use it in one of two meanings (1) special or concrete, as the history of the earth, of plants, of vertebrates, of the law of real property, of the English people. Here the subject-matter is in each case limited, as it must be in any work save a history of the universe. In practice we limit the word to subjects directly connected with the political experience of the human race. This is an arbitrary limitation: but far more arbitrary is the division into periods, as Ancient, Mediaeval, and Modern. The other meaning is when it is employed (2) to express 'historical study.' Here we are concerned not with matter but with method. The notion is quite a general one and the term is abstract.

In the former sense a particular history may be learnt, that is, its matter may be more or less completely assimilated and retained. In the latter, the methods may be more or less thoroughly acquired as a science and practised as an art. In the former it is mainly the quantity, in the latter it is the quality, that makes the difference between one student and another.

Historical study is applied Logic. Reasoning is applied (1) to the appraising of evidence, that is, to the extraction of fact, (2) to the appraising of facts, that is, to the extraction of their meaning.

Now the further events are removed from us the harder it is as a rule to ascertain the truth about them. The nearer they are to us the harder it is as a rule to gauge their significance.

It is not necessary to prove what has been called the 'unity of history.' The continuity of the history of mankind is not now questioned, and it is more and more established by the extension of research. We cannot ignore progress, however at times concealed or checked. But, since human powers are limited, it is usual to fix the historical eye upon a group of peoples in whose history progress is clearly seen. The history with which we habitually deal is 'European' history, the history of a group of progressive peoples who live or lived in or who came recently from Europe. Its roots reach as far as India and its branches are spreading over every sea.

If this be the history with which we are dealing, and if we are for convenience sake to divide it into three great periods, it is only natural to ask what is the meaning of this division, so far as concerns Ancient history. Can it be to any extent justified on grounds other than mere convenience? Can the dividing line or border land be made to coincide with an apparent break of events, a halt and a new departure?

Now History shews us a period in the course of which small city-states, great inorganic kingdoms, rude independent tribes, and one national kingdom (Macedon), share one after another a common destiny. They become parts of an immense organization, the Roman Empire. This is not a true organism, and its dissolution is gradual, a piecemeal process, the converse of its formation. Its Western provinces are formed into kingdoms, the beginnings of the national states of modern times. Here we are in presence of a great contrast. The period in which the separative tendency in the empire overcomes the aggregative is a sort of natural borderland.

Religion presents a not less striking contrast. The old religions are distinctly local, and they are the affairs of groups

—family, clan, state, etc. They are a means of profit, of securing the help of the gods. The gods, great and small, are numberless. Modern religions are (at least potentially) ecumenical, and the affair of the individual. They are (at least in aim) a means of morality, of promoting or checking certain kinds of conduct. They are monotheistic. In European history a natural border-period may be found in the struggles and triumph of the Christian Church.

Nor is it otherwise with Law. It too is an affair of groups and is closely connected with religion. Speaking generally, the ancient state of things is that those who share the same religion (and no others) share the same law. Nowadays this is out of date, at least in Christendom. Law regards individuals, and is not mixed up with religion. Now the period in which it becomes clear that the individual, not the family, is going to be the legal unit, is fairly to be treated as a border-land.

The period that meets these requirements is broadly that from Hadrian to Justinian, more narrowly from Constantine to Justinian, beginning in fact with the failure of the machinery of Diocletian. Into this period students of history, mediaeval and ancient alike, must wander.

Here we must ask, if we limit Ancient History in some such way as this, how is the teaching to be conducted? Has the study of the Ancient period any special objects and methods of its own, primarily connected with it, if not peculiar to it?

Now we know that the history of the Graeco-Roman world is often treated as a part of Classical studies. I have even met with the phrase 'Classical History.' The phrase truly indicates that the 'history' is a mere appendage to the study of the 'Classical' writers. Literary considerations come first, and certain portions of history are forced into prominence. Such are the wretched Peloponnesian war down to 411 B.C. and the Catilinarian conspiracy. Certain other portions are skimmed or skipped, and after the death of Marcus Aurelius the business simply comes to an end. The history of the kingdoms formed out of Alexander's empire is all-important for understanding the connexion of Greek and Roman. But from the Classical point of view its interest suffers: it comes after Demosthenes and before Cicero. In short, the study above sketched is not strictly speaking historical study at all. Facts—'Classical' facts—are tested and verified. This is well done. But the true meaning of the facts is less well grasped, for this 'history' lacks perspective, and affords little help towards judging the relative importance of events. Whence came the men who supplied the enormous demand for all kinds of technical skill created by the Roman Empire? Mostly from the ranks of the 'Hellenistic' Greeks. Where was the chief centre of science and technical skill in the 'Hellenistic' world? Alexandria. Who gave the impulse to this great movement? Aristotle, Alexander, and the early Ptolemies. But the sort of things that the average Classical student will tell you about Alexandria are the story of Caesar swimming with his notebook in one hand, and the amours and tragic end of Cleopatra the sixth. We must of course enter into the spirit of Virgil and Horace (not to mention others) and this we take no small pains to do: but for History as a connected whole, in which the effect of one or more causes is ever becoming a cause of new effects and so on, we are apt to lose both the leisure and the eye.

In short, History must start by looking backward. From consideration of later ages we are enabled to form some notion of the relative importance of events in earlier ages. Even contemporary literature is but a blind guide. It does not as a rule give us bare facts, but merely the writer's view of those facts that seemed to him important. Not to discuss the question of personal bias, the mere omissions are enough to destroy perspective. Nothing is more helpful in illustrating the relations of Athens to her allies than facts concerning the tribute. Yet Thucydides does not tell us of the great increase of the tribute in B.C. 425. The assertions of later orators were naturally discredited by the silence of Thucydides. But in recent years the fragments of an inscription[1] have been found to confirm their assertions. Again, there is a department, Constitutional History, in which the omissions are the rule and clear statement the exception, especially in the case of Rome. Take for instance the popular assemblies. The subject is a byword for obscurity. Nor can we be said to understand the assemblies of the Greek states, save perhaps the Ekklesia of Athens. Is there then no significant fact in relation to primary assemblies that History can extract from the assemblies of Greece and Rome? Yes, surely this much at least, that voting by heads and voting by groups are totally distinct methods of procedure and give wholly different characters to assemblies in which they are respectively used. The group-voting system plays into the hands of the Roman nobles and helps to make the conservative forces dominate in Roman politics. To it is largely due the futility of democratic movements in the last century of the Republic. A Demokraty in the Athenian sense could not exist at Rome : the assembly could only serve to set up a Monarch : and when the Monarch was found, the Monarchy soon made terms with the Senate and ignored the People. In so doing it became permanent. Now this group system is an historical fact of great and manifest importance . it not only influences the destinies of the Roman common-wealth, but it is clearly the outcome of immemorial tendencies and has its roots in the social and political conditions of ancient Italy.

Thus, though Ancient History must and does suffer from the lamentable incompleteness of the record, there is no lack of significant facts on which a cautious teacher may insist. But he must always be looking backward as well as forward, in fact, going forward in order to look backward. In early

[1] See note in Mr Hicks' *Manual* of Greek historical inscriptions, No. 47.

times he is often largely dependent on the help of archaeology and comparative philology and mythology. Studies of ancient law and custom have been even more fruitful. The 'method of survivals' has in judicious hands been a means of suggestion and correction. On the other hand the bulk of documentary evidence is, as compared with that of the later periods, unavoidably small. But in no department of his subject does he find the path more beset with pitfalls than in the critical use of literary testimony. A striking instance of this is the unflagging controversy that still rages over the public careers of Demosthenes and Cicero. To turn to that central figure in the literature of ancient history, Polybius. His varied and practical experience of public affairs, his Greek and Roman connexions, his wide and philosophic views of history, all render him a writer of first-rate importance. Yet his opinions are sometimes grievously narrow and one-sided. He judges Demosthenes by an unfair standard, and his views of former Greek politics are coloured by Achaean jealousy of the Sparta of a later day. At the same time he misreads the working of the Roman constitution and needs himself the excuse of what I may call contemporary blindness, the very justice that he refuses to Demosthenes. We are perhaps in less danger of being misled by the Roman writers. Their bias is as a rule too manifest. Livy is preoccupied with the glory of Rome, Tacitus sees the Empire through Senatorial glasses. We are perhaps even tempted now and then to discount their utterances too freely. But, of all ancient historians, the one on whom it is hardest to exercise a sound judgment is Thucydides. His weighty seriousness (not to mention other qualities) is apt to disconcert criticism. For instance, we learn much indirectly from his speeches, but we treat them as mainly his own compositions made to suit certain characters and certain occasions. We are tempted to think that his use of fiction based on inference ends with these set orations. But, if we turn to the story of Alcibiades' influence on Tissaphernes, we see the same method more subtilly disguised. Here are two arrant rogues in conference. That a third person was admitted is surely quite inconceivable. The account must either come from one of the principals, neither of whom was likely to tell the truth with honest intent : or from inference drawn by the writer or his direct informant. The context[1] of the passage (viii. 46) makes the latter alternative highly probable. We may perhaps conclude that, even in Thucydides, what seems to be a narrative of attested facts may now and then be little more than acute, and probably correct, inference. In short, high literary qualities and trustworthy historical evidence are things wholly distinct : and this truism can never be too constantly borne in mind by the teacher or student of Ancient History.

Speaking of literature reminds us of the most important of all the departments of history, the history of Thought. Intellectual and political movements are always acting and reacting on each other, and the continuity of history is sometimes most clearly seen in intellectual movements that do not for a long time appear on the surface of political life. They commonly have a moral side, and what touches life in the long run touches politics. Hence the immense interest of the early Greek Sophists. Here we find the beginnings of that long questioning of Man, of the State, of popular theology and popular morals, that ends in cosmopolitanism and a practical monotheism. The way is being prepared for the recognition of one great emperor on earth and one great God in heaven. The individual is beginning to assert himself, and the narrow city patriotism of the Greek enters on a period of sad but necessary decay. Great movements such as this find insufficient notice in ordinary manuals of history. They go on over so great a space of time, and spread over so wide an area, that it is hard to keep the attention fixed on them, and they commonly receive only scattered reference in the separate histories of Greece and Rome. There is work here for a teacher to do.

[1] Chapters 87-8 should also be read in connexion with this passage.

If he does no more than make fairly clear the enormous power of Greek influences in Roman life and Roman history from the age of the Gracchi to the age of the Antonines, he will have done what is worth doing. He will have to treat of men of action as well as men of thought : and with the writer and the teacher he will have to place the freedman and the slave. He will range from theories of virtue to the ministry of pleasures : he will see the Roman love of precedent and order combining with wider views and a scientific bent, and the result a gradual reform of Law. He will have to illustrate the subtle variety of Greek influences in the case of such contemporaries as Cicero and Atticus, Cato and Brutus, and last not least in the clearsighted and serene cosmopolitanism of Julius Caesar.

It is often asked, when should Ancient History be supposed to begin? Can a practical line be drawn? Archaeology overlaps what we can strictly call History, but it goes much further back : it revels in the 'prehistoric.' So tóo Anthropology, of which in its widest sense History is but a branch. I must ask indulgence for an attempt to fix the beginning of History proper by the criterion of our beginning to know something of a people's thoughts and ideals. This view may derive support from the deep interest so long taken in the great 'Homeric question.' That interest does not shew much sign of flagging. We long to know whose voice or voices are speaking to us. How much is due to imagination, how much is a picture of real life? What are the approximate dates of the poems? What age do they profess to represent? And so on, question after question. Surely we feel that the history of the Greeks is beginning for us, when we read what the Greeks themselves treasured as the earliest voices of their race.

The first and most obvious use of the study of Ancient History is that it prepares the way for an intelligent study of later times. It has, however, in and for itself, a high educational value. The very defects of record that often make a certain conclusion unattainable are from this point of view a recommendation. Doubtful footing calls for careful walking, and the cautious inferences and frequent suspension of judgment unavoidable in Ancient History render it undeniably helpful in the training of a sober mind. Fair abilities and a sound elementary education must of course be presupposed in the student. History belongs rather to the later than to the earlier stages of a wholesome educational scheme. I shall decline the impertinence of offering general advice to teachers. Let me rather conclude with the harmless commonplace that as the teacher cannot do without books so books cannot at present do without the man.

THE TEACHING OF ECONOMIC HISTORY.

1. By the publication of the *Wealth of Nations* Adam Smith convinced the English public that Political Economy had a right to an independent place in the circle of the sciences; in a similar way it was through the work of James Edward Thorold Rogers that Economic History came to be recognized in England as a separate branch of investigation. His monumental *History of Agriculture and Prices*, together with such special studies as the *First Nine Years of the Bank of England*, forced men to feel that the abundant materials he made available had been too long neglected; while his *Six Centuries* and *Economic Interpretation of History* shewed that the new method of investigation might throw much fresh suggestion and interesting side-lights on the most familiar periods of English history. Before his epoch-making work on Agriculture and Prices appeared, these questions had been regarded by English writers as an interesting topic for occasional and incidental remark; but he demonstrated effectively that this subject is deserving of the serious attention it now receives from the general historian, and that it demands separate and independent treatment, so that its bearing may be properly brought out.

2. There had been various causes at work which had rendered Englishmen less ready than Continental scholars to attempt to remedy their neglect of the economic side of national

life[1]. Historians were apt to leave such phenomena on one side, because they found so little material in the sources to which they habitually turned. The facts about economic changes have often been recorded, but they are rarely chronicled. The changes from natural to money economy, and the rise of a class of free labourers in England, were slow processes extending over many centuries. These movements were for the most part so gradual that they eluded the observation of contemporary writers. They were, moreover, movements that were brought about unconsciously, and cannot be ascribed to the deliberate policy of any known individual, and they are therefore unassociated with any great name. The personal element was for the most part lacking; and the annalist, who recorded the doings of men, was apt to treat economic affairs as the mere setting of a drama that derived its interest from the play of passion and the triumph of the strong man or the wise ruler. The chronicles published by the Master of the Rolls rarely furnished the necessary data; and even when they happened to include occasional reference to economic affairs, it was difficult for the modern student to find a clue to the meaning of the incidents recorded. Nor could the student of history obtain much help in this matter from the English economists. The classical school, with Mill as its last representative, professed to study the facts of modern society; it was only on the assumption of free competition that their principles and terminology would apply, or that, as they held, any economic science was possible. It was thus that they dismissed the conditions of earlier days to a supposed age of custom as a dreary limbo which the light of science could never hope to penetrate. There were, of course, authors like Finlay, who had a keen insight into the economic side of human affairs; but quotations of prices, and market regulations and financial expedients were for the most part such

[1] Compare my article *Why had Roscher so Little Influence in England?* in the *Annals of the American Academy of Political Science*, 1894.

unintelligible details that the historian was apt to put them on one side, while the economist could not give effective aid in the effort to analyse, to describe and to coordinate such obscure phenomena.

3. Both from the nature of the recorded information on which we have to rely and from the character of the results sought for, Economic History must be dealt with as a separate branch of study, if it is to be properly treated at all. To make this claim is not to advocate any revolutionary change in the conception of History as a whole. We may plead for the careful and thorough examination of this one aspect, without forgetting that it is only an aspect; or even without contending that this has in itself more importance than other lines of historical research. Economic History deals with the physical side of the life of communities and of individuals : it dwells on the practical use and misuse of national resources, and the successes and failures due to financial experiments; and it brings into prominence the fundamental influence in social affairs of the need of food and shelter and the requirements which man feels in common with lower animals. For many of us, however, the chief attraction of historical study is due to the elements that are distinctively human; it lies in the growth of polities, in the institutions for administering justice and for organizing mutual defence, in personal aims and national aspirations and the effort to realize them. There is doubtless the closest connexion and interrelation between the institutional or religious development of a people and its material progress; but after all, the Body Politic, with the institutions by which free men govern themselves, is a more admirable creation of Reason than the Economic Organism in which men cater for each other's needs. The development of the State is the final object of research; but the more thoroughly we apply ourselves to political and constitutional history, the more necessary will it be at every point to take account of the results obtained by the study of Economic History. We may

devote ourselves to this branch of work not as an end in itself, but because we regard it as a necessary means for getting a clearer view of the actual development of the State. We may recognise its real importance without regarding it as supreme; we may take account of economic forces, while we decline to admit that the pressure of physical needs has been the main factor in determining the course of human affairs[1].

4. Economic History, though not of paramount or exclusive importance, yet rightly claims the serious attention of students. It brings into light the reasons for military or political action that would otherwise be obscure, and thus helps to render the whole course of human affairs more intelligible. The failure of Charles V.'s schemes for the maintenance of the ancient *régime* in Germany and his personal loss of *prestige*, were directly due to the exhaustion of his credit with the Fuggers of Augsburg. The financial difficulties of the papacy in the fifteenth century had not a little to do with the widespread sale of indulgences and the scandals which roused Luther to action. Economic analysis invariably has the effect of turning the attention from that which lies on the surface to the deeper influences that are less easily observed. These forces are all the more potent because their action is often gradual and sometimes cumulative; it is easy for the student to leave them out of sight till the description of some sudden crisis forces them on his notice; but it is necessary to take account of the beginnings and stages in Economic development if we would understand constitutional changes and foreign and domestic policy. Industrial and commercial affairs must for convenience sake be treated apart, but they cannot be omitted, if the course of History is to be rendered intelligible and the study is to be conducted in a scientific spirit.

When we once take our stand consciously on the economic platform we are able, with comparatively little effort, to get into close touch with the men of past ages. There is often a

[1] Cunningham, *Growth of Industry and Commerce*, I. 12.

strange sense of bewilderment in studying the religious ideas
or even the moral judgments current in bygone times; the
influence of omens on the fortunes of war in ancient days is
unintelligible to us; the contrast between the high ideals and
the grossness of medieval life is a shock to our sensibility; and
even in modern days we are confused by the different conceptions of liberty and justice which are found in different countries.   But the practical problems which men have to face are
very similar in all ages : the chief requirements of human life,
food, shelter and clothing, involve the use of the same products and a similar struggle with nature; the husbandry and
cattle-breeding of different peoples are alike; the industrial
arts—mining and smelting, spinning and weaving—have only
undergone considerable change in countries where the era of
invention has made its mark.   With a little effort we can place
ourselves in thought on the industrial level of primitive man.
So, too, wherever the use of money and the development of
credit have come into vogue at all they have had analogous
effects on commercial practice.   Indeed, we may press the
matter further and say that the forms of economic organization
which have been developed among different peoples are singu-
larly alike; the household, as a social unit with no economic
independence in its parts, is found in all ages, though the
functions it subserves have been greatly restricted in modern
times; city life, with its enormous resources, and its possibilities of administrative corruption, has been a feature common
to all high civilizations.   In their ideals and aspirations men differ
fundamentally; but the touch of practical necessity makes the
whole world kin; the limitations imposed by physical needs
are similar for all peoples; the opportunities afforded by natural
resources in one age resemble those offered in another, though
there is a growth in the power of appreciating and using them.
The organs and the methods which human society has developed at different times for dealing with industrial problems
are closely analogous.   Hence, while the historian must often

treat of things that are unfamiliar, he will find that in this practical sphere the habits and institutions of the past have much in common with affairs that lie within present day experience. The economic interpretation of history not only helps to call attention to underlying tendencies, but brings the men of the distant past on to a plane where we can, if we try, enter most closely into their interests and find their action thoroughly comprehensible.

5. To the student of the past economic research offers many advantages, not only in the assistance it may give in interpreting particular epochs and incidents, but from the manner in which it presents the continuity of History. Man's enthusiasms and opinions and passions are subject to frequent, and sometimes violent change ; but in so far as his relations to his physical environment are concerned, his activities must be steadily maintained from month to month and year to year. Each season the grain has been sowed and the harvest reaped with more or less success : there has been no break in the recurrence of agricultural operations or of industrial life. So too, the lines of communication which have once been opened by trade are not easily interrupted, but serve after long ages for the intercourse of peoples and the transmission of culture. These physical conditions remain very much the same ; and the constitution of human society, in so far as it is organized with reference to these matters, has a remarkable persistence. There has been a perpetuation of the manual arts from sheer necessity, and a transmission of particular forms of skill among new peoples, as well as a transplanting of institutions that are congruent with particular phases of industrial life. This process has involved constant adaptation and modification : but, till a century ago, it has been a gradual readjustment without sudden breaks or violent changes[1]. By no other line of historical

[1] The age of geographical discovery may be taken as the exception that proves the rule, and it was only brought about through long and conscious effort.

study is the continuity of human history and the organic connexion of the past and present so clearly exhibited.

6. To the man of affairs Economic History may prove of interest from quite another reason—by furnishing a clue to unfamiliar habits and practice in the present day. The expansion of Western Civilization has brought Europeans and Americans into the closest contact with many barbarous and half-civilized peoples, whose usages and habits are strange to us. For purposes of trade it is convenient to understand their methods of dealing; while the administrator who rules over them cannot easily see how the incidence of taxation will be distributed in their communities or what are the possibilities of social oppression against which it is necessary to guard. Some of the most regrettable blunders of the English government in India have been due to an inability to understand the working of native institutions. A careful study of the past of our own race, or of the earlier habits of other peoples when natural economy still reigned, would at least have suggested a point of view from which the practical problems in India might be more wisely looked at. By means of analogies drawn from the past we may come to understand the advantage, under certain circumstances, of fiscal methods that seem to be cumbrous, and the danger of introducing modern improvements in a polity that is not prepared to assimilate them.

7. Since the teaching of Economic History as an independent branch of study has been so recently introduced, there has hardly been enough experience to warrant any definite conclusions about the best methods of instruction, especially as the subject belongs to different groups in the curricula of different Universities. At Harvard, in the new Cambridge, it is treated as a branch of Economics, and attended by those who have some familiarity with modern Economics; in the old Cambridge it is hardly taken up by the best economic students at all, while it forms a part of the regular course for the Historical Tripos, though it is not a necessary subject in

that department. It appears, however, that there are three lines of inquiry which the student should be encouraged to pursue, if he is to be properly equipped for making use of this branch of knowledge, either in connexion with historical research or in the practical business of life.

a. It seems desirable that he should become acquainted with the economic development of some one particular country from its earliest beginnings. The change from natural to money economy and its effects can be examined most clearly when the field is limited; the various social organisms,—such as the household, the city, and the nation,—can be best comprehended in their several characters, and their mutual relations can be most easily understood when they are seen in a limited area. The various economic institutions,—merchant gilds, and misteries, staples, and regulated companies,—may be treated with greater precision when they are separated from analogous but different associations. And if one country is to be thus selected it is clear that England has special claims to be taken as the type. The mass of recorded evidence which is available in England is very large, and there is extant information on many points that cannot apparently be treated with the same definiteness in other lands. England is so far isolated by her position that it is possible to trace her debt to other countries with comparative certainty, while the rapidity and the extent of the growth of her industrial prosperity make English history an appropriate field for observing this line of progress. English Economic History, as giving the type of the actual development of one society, is a natural basis for all instruction in this department.

b. It is also necessary that the student should have an acquaintance with economic terminology and be habituated to economic analysis, so as to have the means of describing the phenomena of the past and of stating the economic causes of growth or decay. The Classical Economists were at no pains to state their doctrines in a form in which they could be of service to the investigator of history; they concentrated their attention on modern society and assumed the existence of free competition in formulating their principles; and they were consequently unable to provide the necessary phraseology for discussing other phases of human progress. But they did not say the last word. Modern Economists have discarded this restriction, and endeavour to enlarge the subject-matter of the science and to take account of the human race in all stages of its progress[1]. Even for the thorough understanding of the special conditions to which the classical writers confined their attention, it is necessary to include a large range of phenomena which they ignored. Since Economists have begun to treat modern problems in their proper place as the most recent phase of a long-continued process, they have gradually provided a scientific economic terminology which is directly applicable to bygone times.

c. The student who is acquainted with one concrete type of economic development, and has an adequate nomenclature at his command, should be encouraged to enlarge his knowledge by studying other societies, and especially to obtain a survey in outline of the contribution of each people to the economic history of the world. He may thus get a clearer grasp of the institutions with which he has already become acquainted, by comparing them with their analogues; he will trace the action of similar causes in different places or at different times, and thus gauge their importance more truly, while he will get a clearer view of the unity of history and of the part which each people has played in the progress of the race[2].

8. From the foregoing paragraphs it will have already

---

[1] K. Bücher, *Entstehung*, 8.

[2] Each of these topics has formed part of the regular instruction in Cambridge; and for each I have attempted to provide a small text-book, (*a*) *Outlines of English Industrial History* (with E. A. McArthur), (*b*) *Modern Civilisation in its Economic Aspects*, (*c*) *Western Civilisation*.

appeared that in the opinion of the writer, Economic History is not a branch of learning which can be wisely included in a school course. There are of course many economic phenomena which may be usefully attended to by the teacher; but the subject is deficient in direct human interest, and deals with the deeper and less obvious causes of change; it may well be deferred till it can be entered on as a subject of academic study. And it has much to offer which renders it a valuable medium of instruction at the University; it necessarily brings the student face to face with many problems in the weighing of evidence; it forces him to feel the supreme importance of documents as a source of information, and to realize the difficulties in interpreting them aright. It may also prove of value in rousing the interest of students in their work, by bringing them into closer touch with the men of bygone days—their methods of work and habits of business. In so far as it renders the past less bookish, and by shewing us men engaged in familiar pursuits makes it more vivid, the economic aspect of history may prove attractive to beginners who find the development of constitutional liberties comparatively uninspiring. Lastly, it may be pointed out that it offers an ample field for students to make their first essays in planning and carrying out an original investigation. From the very fact that Economic History has only recently received due recognition there are many points in this branch of research which demand much fuller examination than ·they have yet received; and some of these can be usefully dealt with in moderate compass. The inquirer, who has a little skill and patience at command, may hope to find a definite task on which to try his unaided powers, and the subject that attracts him most is likely to be that in which he will do his best. When viewed from this standpoint, we may see that the Economic History is proving an admirable medium for the self-education of those who have taken their degrees and desire to pursue their studies further. The former students of the Cambridge Historical School have compiled during the last ten years a considerable number of interesting monographs, and their work in the field of Economic History has been productive of some results that are likely to prove of permanent value.   The method of training has been tentative, and it will doubtless be greatly improved by longer experience ; but when tried by this test it seems to have had a measure of success.

THE TEACHING OF
CONSTITUTIONAL HISTORY[1].

To those who hold that history is one and indivisible, to speak of constitutional history is an offence. If Freeman said that there was no such thing as ancient history, his successors protest against ecclesiastical, constitutional, economic, or military history. The extremists go so far as to refuse us national history, and would make the true standpoint of the historian international.

The position is at any rate an arguable one. It is a matter of vital importance in our national history that England was for centuries consciously a part of the Church Universal, and it may be said that the historian should not be encouraged to relegate this fact and its vast consequences to a separate volume. The history of the Church is closely connected with the history of the constitution, and that again with the history of industry. Military history can scarcely be treated apart from State policy, and in some periods dynastic history seems at first sight almost to cover the whole ground.

But what is philosophically desirable is not always practically possible, and though the historian can sometimes afford to be a philosopher, the teacher of history must be a man of business.

[1] The writer desires gratefully to acknowledge the suggestive criticism of Mr Stanley M. Leathes, of Trinity College, Cambridge, to whom this chapter was submitted in manuscript.

4—2

Experience shews that as a matter of business subdivision is essential, and we can quote against the philosophers one of themselves. 'Above all things,' says Bacon[1], 'order, and distribution, and singling out of parts, is the life of despatch : so as the distribution be not too subtile ; for he that doth not divide will never enter well into business, and he that divideth too much will never come out of it clearly.' English constitutional history is by tradition the backbone of the Cambridge Historical Tripos, and a continuous experience of many years has próved that it can be taught efficiently as a subject by itself, without the separation doing violence to the sense of proportion, or obscuring its true relation to the larger subject of which it is a part.

In the Cambridge school division has indeed been carried further, and English constitutional history has itself been divided at A.D. 1485, the earlier subject being assigned to Part I. of the Tripos, and the later to Part II. This involves their being taught in different years and by different lecturers. Perhaps A.D. 1485 originally became the landmark because it was the point at which Stubbs ended and Hallam began, but without venturing to dispute the question with the high authorities who prefer A.D. 1509, we may hold that the separation between medieval and modern history may be looked for not very far from this point. The reign of Henry VII. marks the surrender of feudal decentralisation to the forces of government, and the end of private war. It is true that Green places his 'new monarchy' earlier and makes Henry VII. an imitator of Edward IV., but Edward IV.'s reign left the factions unreconciled and the dynastic quarrel still alive, while Henry VII.'s claim to be the founder of a new monarchy rests on the achievement of a united kingdom, an assured succession, and independence of foreign interference. The influence of the Renaissance and the New Learning point

---

[1] *Essays Civil and Moral*, xxv. 'Of Despatch.'

in the same direction. The discovery of the New World was making it no longer possible to believe that the whole drama of human action had been played on a narrow stage. This one event, as has been pointed out often enough, must have involved a reconstruction of men's ways of thinking analogous to that which was to take place later in a different sphere, when the Copernican theories revealed the immense extension of the Universe in space, and the relative insignificance of the planet which had hitherto been deemed the only world, lying under its 'majestical roof fretted with golden fire.' And it was just now that the printing-press was beginning to admit the many to share the speculations of the few. Thus, in spite of the survival of chivalry at the English Court—the accounts of Hall and Holinshed read like the *Morte d'Arthur*[1]— Henry VII. and his son may be classed as modern princes. Even the notion of the expansion of England begins with the

---

[1] 'On the first day of May the king, accompanied with many lusty bachelors on great and well-doing horses, rode to the wood to fetch May; where a man might have seen many a horse raised on high, with carrier, gallop, turn, and stop, marvellous to behold....And as they were returning on the hill a ship met with them under sail. The master hailed the king and that noble company, and said that he was a mariner, and was come from many a strange port, and came thither to see if any deeds of arms were to be done in the country, of the which he might make true report in other countries.' The ship is called *Fame*, and is laden with '*good Renown.*' 'Then said the herald : If you will bring your ship into the bay of *Hardiness* you must double the point of *Gentleness*, and there you shall see a company that will meddle with your merchandise. Then said the king: Sithens Renown is their merchandise let us buy it if we can. Then the ship shot a peal of guns, and sailed forth before the king's company full of flags and banners till it came to the tiltyard....Then began the trumpets to sound and the horses to run, that many a spear was brast and many a great stripe given....On the third day the queen made a great banket to the king and all them that had justed; and after the banket done she gave the chief prize to the king, the second to the Earl of Essex, the third to the Earl of Devonshire, and the fourth to the lord Marquess Dorset. Then the heralds cried: My lords, for your noble feats in arms God send you the love of your ladies that you most desire.' (*Holinshed*, p. 809).

Tudors, and Lord Herbert of Cherbury makes the statesmen of 1511 say : 'When we would enlarge ourselves let it be that way we can, and to which it seems the Eternal Providence hath destined us ; which is, by sea'[1].

But it is not suggested that the division of constitutional history for purposes of teaching into two halves is ideally the best method.   The considerations that make it necessary are at bottom practical considerations.   Just as in research the medievalist and the modernist are inevitable products of needful specialisation, so in teaching it is scarcely possible that the whole of English constitutional history should be thoroughly well done by one man—at any rate if University standards are to be maintained.

From the teacher's point of view it is a notable fact that of late years English constitutional history has become at once more interesting and of higher educational value.   If recollections of the undergraduate's standpoint as it was twenty years ago are to be trusted, the earlier part of the subject was deposited in three sacred volumes, which were approached by the devout disciple in much the same spirit as that in which the youthful Brahmin draws near to the Vedas.   To read the first volume of Stubbs was necessary to salvation ; to read the second was greatly to be desired ; the third was reserved for the ambitious student who sought to accumulate merit by unnatural austerities—but between them they covered the whole ground.   The lecturer lectured on Stubbs ; the commentator elucidated him ; the crammer boiled him down. Within those covers was to be found the final word on every controversy, and in this faith the student moved serene.

Had our classic been less learned, less comprehensive, less profound, such a superstition could scarcely have grown up round a single treatise, but it was a beneficent superstition while it lasted, and not a few of the generation now middle-

[1] *Life and Reign of King Henry the Eighth*, 18.

aged can trace back their first notion of what is meant by the judicial treatment of a complex case to a reverential study of Stubbs's *Constitutional History*. But controversy has its uses in education, and it is not good that all questions should be settled in advance by authority. An exposition of the reasons why *A* is wrong may be of more educational value than a statement of the fact that *B* is right, and it is fortunate that recent research in this subject has increased the number of questions that may be debated and has at the same time intensified the interest of the debates. What were once the official views have been attacked, and brilliantly attacked, at many points. By the *History of English Law*, and *Domesday Book and Beyond*, to say nothing of *Roman Canon Law in the Church of England*, and his other contributions to legal history, Professor Maitland has laid students of the English constitution under obligations that are incalculable. Mr Horace Round has revolutionised our views on knight service, the hundred, and a variety of kindred matters. Other writers have exhibited the extraordinary difficulty of questions that once seemed to belong to the category of problems solved. It has been the business of the teachers to bring the new knowledge to bear on the old conclusions, and to shew how far and why these are to be modified, and the result has been to create a new atmosphere of criticism in the lecture-room. It is perhaps fanciful to detect a difference in the educational product, and to suggest that under the new order the student has become more inquiring, more acute, and less easily satisfied with the regular formulæ.

Ever since the beginning the Cambridge school has set great store by the study of documents, and this we owe to the early pioneers. For many years Stubbs's *Select Charters* was the corner-stone of the structure, though as the volume did not deal with the 14th and 15th centuries, supplied no detailed comment, and might easily be strengthened, especially in pre-Norman periods, a good deal was left for the teacher to do.

Then came Dr S. R. Gardiner's *Constitutional Documents of the Puritan Revolution*, 1625—1660 ; and not long after Dr G. W. Prothero published *Statutes and Constitutional Documents*, 1559—1625, with its full and suggestive Introduction.   The Reformation statutes are be found in *Documents illustrative of English Church History*, compiled by Mr H. Gee and Mr W. J. Hardy, but a convenient volume of papers for the Restoration and Hanoverian periods is yet to seek.   With the original papers actually at hand it is possible to achieve something remotely analogous to laboratory work, and to illustrate the processes by which history is really made.   At the same time the ancient phrases and the conceptions of other days help to furnish a background and an atmosphere to the young historian.   In this way better than in obedience to express precept the conviction with which he starts is gradually abandoned that all historical problems are capable of being stated in terms of Victorian politics.

Nevertheless it is important that the teacher of constitutional history, while appreciating the need of antiquarian research, should also be on his guard against its dangers.   It is necessary as an aid and a commentary, but it should not be allowed to become the principal subject of interest and study.   It is scarcely too much to say that there are things which a student must be told, but which it is most undesirable that he should make an effort to remember.   For instance, if the teacher explains to him the exact nature of the writ *praecipe* and of 'prerogative wardship,' it should not be with a view to his retaining their technicalities in his mind, but rather to illustrate and make more real the relation between the King and the under-lords.   The chief difficulty is that of satisfying the need for solidity and connectedness without overburdening the memory.   This last danger is increased by the fact that the principal authorities for early constitutional history are laws and edicts.   This sets up a tendency to wander too far into legal matters, instead of devoting this wasted energy to an attempt to understand the conditions under which these laws and edicts worked, and the manner of their administration. It is true that it may be impossible to discover these, but the attempt must be made, and until it has been made it is dangerous to accept a law as an ultimate, dominating fact, as if it were a nineteenth century statute.

Another point of importance to the teacher—especially to the teacher of earlier constitutional history—is the necessity of accentuating the difference between medieval habits of mind and life and modern. It is desirable that the student should learn to sympathise with Becket, and even with Richard II.; it is not good that he should side as a partisan, even with Simon de Montfort. The natural tendency to become enthusiastic over liberal and modern movements in medieval history is so strong that the teacher will do wisely to lay stress, even to exaggeration, upon the fundamental differences.

It may not be superfluous to mention also the risk which the student of earlier constitutional history runs of substituting words and expressions for ideas. Absolute darkness often lurks behind the easy use of such phrases as 'feudal,' 'manorial,' 'parliamentary,' 'representative,' and yet it is possible by the use of them to make an appearance of knowledge. It will be part of the business of the judicious teacher to expose these impostures, and to make sure that the terms sum up knowledge instead of serving as a substitute for it. He will also be careful to realise the necessity of clearly distinguishing facts that are ascertained, from inferences which however probable are not certain. The immature student aches for a dogma and yearns for simplicity. He must learn by painful repetition that dogmatic assertion about the facts of medieval history is too often false, and that medieval life was hardly more simple than modern.

There is another danger that arises where the teaching of a subject like English constitutional history becomes too merely antiquarian. The student who investigates origins and machinery may easily lose his sense of proportion, and cease to appreciate the relation of his special department to all that

lies outside it.   In Cambridge a corrective to this is found in
the still unexhausted influence of Seeley among the teachers
who were once his pupils.   His habit was to seek for tendencies
and causes.   He preferred what he called 'large considerations,' and was more at home in dealing with a century than a
decade.   The whole drift of his mind was towards the suggestive treatment of large phenomena rather than the minute
investigation of details.   His most characteristic course of
lectures as Regius Professor of Modern History was one on
the Holy Roman Empire, delivered in the academical year
1879–80, in which he began with the fall of Rome before the
barbarians and ended with a lecture on the characteristics of
modern democracy.   Thus it would be difficult for a pupil of
Seeley's, while dealing with a department and expounding the
importance of documents, to lose touch altogether with the
general course of events in history.   In describing the Church
settlement of Elizabeth, for instance, a teacher of this school
would not be content with the Acts of Supremacy and Uni-
formity and the terms of the Prayer-book and the Articles.
He would point out that the Church of Elizabeth was an island
Church, as unlike the Churches of Zürich and Geneva on
the one side as she was to the Church of Rome on the other—
the Prayer-book gathered from ancient sources, the tone
of her devotion widely different from the spirit of continental
Church worship, the 'organic relation with Catholic antiquity'
carefully preserved.   As one has well said, the Church of
Elizabeth was isolated 'from the rest of Christendom,
and cut off from the flow of its religious thought. She was
not Catholic, as countries which accepted the decrees of
the Council of Trent understood Catholicism; still less was
she Protestant, as Calvin or William the Silent understood
Protestantism[1].'   It is a narrow view that rules out of the
province of the teacher of constitutional history general facts
of this order of importance.   He is concerned primarily, it is

[1] H. O. Wakeman, *The Church and the Puritans*, p. 11.

true, with the constitutional machinery of the Church, but it is essential that he should deal, however briefly, with the place of the Church in the order of Christendom, and her relation to the other bodies which the Reformation created.

To take another illustration—the teacher of English constitutional history is mainly concerned with the causes which led to the Revolution of 1688, the curious quasi-legal procedure by which it was effected, and its immediate and ultimate results upon the constitution of the 18th century. But the Revolution was also an event of the utmost importance in European history, an episode in the conflict with Louis XIV. William of Orange did not come to England as William the Conqueror came—to obtain for himself a better inheritance. His expedition was in a manner a daring attempt to occupy one of the vital strategic positions in the battlefield of Europe—to appropriate the resources and fleet of England for the benefit of the combination against France.

The point is that though as a matter of business it is convenient to teach history by departments, it is not well that the teacher should be troubled by too fine a sense of relevance. The development of institutions may be his main concern, but he must not lose sight of the relation of the parts to the whole. Thus in spite of his documents and his antiquarianism, he is not cut off from the great, the stirring, the dramatic aspects of history. He is not so completely absorbed in musty records that he has no eye for the great elemental forces. It is therefore possible for his work to stimulate thought and imagination as well as to promote accuracy. Though vitally interested in the minutiæ of his subject, he finds himself also concerned with 'large considerations.' This perhaps is the answer to the question how constitutional history can be brought to bear effectively upon the average student, who is suspicious of documents and is apt to be bored by details. If the teaching is pedantic and narrow, history is a lost cause with him. If it gives him a reason for his work, explains to what purpose facts are to be mastered, exhibits the relation of his subject to the general drift of things, there is a fair chance that the dull imagination may be quickened and the dry bones may live.

It is good that the teacher of constitutional history should look beyond the limits of his department, but it is also good that he should allow his mind to play freely within it. While avoiding what is fanciful, he must keep an open mind for analogies and contrasts that are really suggestive. These are specially to be desired after the death of Queen Anne, when the reign of dulness sets in. The ultimate dependence of the Prime Minister upon Parliament is a point that gains in interest if it is contrasted with the days when a minister, unless supported by a popular rising, depended wholly upon the king, so that for Wolsey it was as true as for the Eastern vizier that 'in the light of the king's countenance' was life, and his wrath 'as messengers of death[1].' And the same official's supreme position and monopoly of affairs is the more striking when we are reminded that it was made a matter of complaint against Buckingham in Charles I.'s reign that he was—what the modern Prime Minister is recognised to be—a 'monopolist of counsels,' a 'blazing star very exorbitant in the affairs of this Commonwealth.'

The habit of allowing the mind thus to range freely over a great area is not without its perils for weaker students. Superficial generalisation, the hunt for distant analogies, the eloquent development of misleading contrasts—these have a dangerous fascination; and a pernicious taste for the dramatic may be easily acquired. But constitutional history is heavily ballasted with facts, and it is impossible to make a fair show in it without

[1] Brewer points out that it is when the king first frowns on him that Shakespeare makes Wolsey say :

> 'I have touched the highest point of all my greatness ;
> And from that full meridian of my glory
> I haste now to my setting: I shall fall
> Like a bright exhalation in the evening,
> And no man see me more.'

some solid reading. Thus the risks are on the whole far less than in some other subjects, and after all it is possible to sacrifice too much to safety, for the best things are missed by those who refuse to leave the beaten track. We cannot afford to neglect any reasonable means of rousing the interest and stimulating the imagination, and what helps the stronger men to firmness of grasp and independence of judgment must not be set on one side in the supposed interests of the weaker brethren. There are many ways of repressing exuberance, and the nature of the subject will prevent anyone going very far wrong. The teacher of constitutional history is obliged to be systematic; there is no reason why he should not do his best to be suggestive also.

It should be noted in this connexion that in later constitutional history the natural order of treatment is not for the most part chronological. In the Tudor period the Reformation stands as a chapter by itself. Ministers and Council, the Star Chamber, Judicature and Police, the Law of Treason, Ecclesiastical Courts, Local Government, Parliament, Finance, are all capable of treatment in separate lectures. The history of the eighteenth and nineteenth centuries can be dealt with in the same way. Three or four lectures on the changes in the position and power of the Crown since the death of Queen Anne give all that is needed in the way of an outline of events; the rest of the subject can be treated under the history of separate institutions, such as the Prime Minister, the Cabinet, Justice, Parliament, and the like. The seventeenth century, however, presents peculiar difficulties, and requires a different method. The whole character of the period is dramatic, and the story must be allowed to unfold itself according to the order of events. Here the separate treatment of institutions will be abandoned, and the lectures will have a different kind of title—Religious Questions under James I., Political Questions under James I., Buckingham and Charles I., Non-parliamentary Government, the Long Parliament and Reform, the Long Parliament and Revolution, the Commonwealth, the Protectorate, the Restoration, the Pension Parliament, the Exclusion Bill, the Revolution.

In planning out a course of lectures on later constitutional history it will be found convenient to preface each of the three main periods by an introductory lecture, avoiding details and giving a preliminary survey of the ground. In the first of these something may be said of the conditions under which the Tudor system came to be established,—of 'livery and maintenance,' the 'eating canker of want' which enfeebled the Lancastrian government, the historical importance of Fortescue, the evidence of the Paston Letters, the humiliation of the baronage after the wars of the Roses, and the dynastic position of the first two Tudor kings. The introductory lecture on the Stuart period would naturally deal with the changed conditions of the seventeenth century as compared with the sixteenth. The danger from great lords and their retainers had passed away, and the long arm of the Privy Council reached into every corner of the kingdom. What men needed now was not protection from the great lords, but protection from the tyranny of the power by which the great lords had been overthrown. The results of the Reformation were now accepted. The long reign of Elizabeth had brought the greater part of the nation into the fold of the Church of England, and the adherents of Rome were only a minority that had ceased to be dangerous. There was no longer any serious danger of foreign invasion, for one result of the Tudor period had been an improvement in the defensible position of England. The successful rebellion of the United Provinces against Spain had placed the ports of Holland in the hands of a friendly Protestant power. Ireland, the 'postern-gate' for Spain, had been reduced to order by the vigorous Viceroys of Elizabeth; the Reformation had separated Scotland from France, and the accession of James I. had united her to England. Thus the England of the Stuarts was an island such as Shakespeare had dreamed of

—compact within itself, 'in a great pool a swan's nest,' 'this precious stone set in the silver sea.' To those who could not foresee the Civil War it must have seemed as if trouble could only come from the Continent—no longer from Scotland, or Ireland, or the 'local disturbances of hostile lords.' A danger of Elizabeth's reign had been a disputed succession, but the Stuart House succeeded without opposition; and unlike the childless Tudors the Stuarts were 'enriched' with 'a most royal progeny of most rare and excellent gifts and forwardness.' Yet the race that now inherited the Crown of England was politically inferior, and at a time when the changed conditions required the highest and most far-seeing statesmanship, its members displayed qualities of only the ordinary type. Meanwhile a rival power had been growing up that was ready to take their authority out of their hands. One of the great achievements of the Tudor period had been the consolidation of Parliamentary institutions, and in Parliament the House of Commons was becoming the most important factor, for the country gentry and the commercial classes had been elevated into political importance. And if Parliament had grown strong enough in the sixteenth century to be a rival to the Crown should need arise, in the seventeenth century powerful motives began to operate to induce Parliament to take up an independent attitude—motives arising out of two questions of the first importance, taxation and religion. Yet there was nothing revolutionary about the tone of the earlier Parliamentary leaders. It was not Pym and Hampden who were the Jacobins of the Great Rebellion. Their business was to deal with isolated abuses, and they did not realise at once that their attacks upon individual grievances were taking shape in a coherent policy, which was destined in the long run to transfer the ultimate sovereignty from the Crown to Parliament, and so to shift the centre of gravity of the State. There is no eager modernness about the statesmen of the Long Parliament. They are not always applying abstract principles, or periodically calling upon ancient institutions to justify their existence. With them 'the novelty' though not rejected, was 'held for a suspect.' If circumstances had allowed them they would have been well content to 'make a stand upon the ancient way.'

The introductory lecture to the 18th and 19th centuries may fairly deal with a variety of general considerations. It might be remarked that the reason why the period is dull to the student of constitutional history is because the striking facts of English history are no longer constitutional facts. The really great achievements of the 18th century are the industrial revolution and the establishment of a world empire beyond sea. The vital matters do not fall within the province of the historian of the constitution ; they belong rather to the economist and the historian of foreign policy, and particularly of war. It should be noted that before the Reform Bill the English system is in the main aristocratic, and an attempt should be made to bring out the importance of the House of Lords in the political organisation, and the predominating influence of individual peers in the composition of the House of Commons. Last of all it should be shewn that what Gneist calls the 'century of Reform and Reform Bills' was inaugurated by an economic and social change, when the rural England of the 17th century, controlled by the country gentry, became the industrial England of the early 19th century, controlled by employers and capitalists. Great towns, as a picturesque French writer puts it, 'shot up and spread with the rapidity of a conflagration, shooting up like flames, and tending ever to engulf each other[1].' The political centre of gravity shifted from the south to the north, and it became inevitable that a constitution which made no provision for the new industrial

[1] Boutmy, *The English Constitution*, p. 185. A note refers to a phrase by Léon Faucher in his *Études sur l'Angleterre:* 'Croissent comme la flamme et ne cessent de tendre vers un abîme de grandeur.'

England should undergo modification. The wonder is not that this was done, but that it was done without a revolution.

Such general considerations as these gain greatly in the force and effectiveness of their presentation if they are expounded in special introductory lectures, instead of being wedged among masses of detail, or appearing from time to time as a digression from the history of particular institutions. In constitutional history the danger of losing sight of the general in the particular is a real one, and if it can be avoided, even at the risk of repetition, the price is not too high.

What has been said of the teacher's method may perhaps be conveniently supplemented at this point by a brief account of the method recommended to the student. One of the virtues most to be desired of him is orderliness; another is the power of seeing things in due proportion, and so of escaping the danger which besets those who lose themselves in detail, and fail to see the wood for the trees. A third is the power of getting at the heart of a book without reading every word of it, but to this beginners should not aspire. "Some books are to be tasted, others to be swallowed, and some few to be chewed and digested: that is, some books are to be read only in parts; others to be read, but not curiously; and some few to be read wholly, and with diligence and attention[1]." But except for the fortunate possessors of Macaulay's memory, what may be called arm-chair reading is, as a rule, worse than useless. The student of history must work pen in hand. It is perhaps best to begin with the largest possible note-book, and enter in it either lecture notes or an analysis of a principal text-book, writing only on one side of the page, and leaving large spaces even there. This gives a general plan of the subject, and into this general plan the results of the subsequent reading should be worked—as analysis, or extracts, or references. Thus into this note-book the fruits of all the student's labours will be garnered, and when the time comes for reviewing

[1] Bacon, *Essays Civil and Moral*, L. 'Of Studies.'

what has been learned, there will be found within its covers all the materials for an orderly revision of the subject. Memory is a good thing, but unless the memory is exceptional, method is better. The man who knows everything is a rare product of education, and after all he is not much better off than the man who knows where everything is to be found. Accurate knowledge of causes and results in general is most often attained by the student who takes the trouble to sort and arrange his details. With rare exceptions the arm-chair reader is inaccurate both in the general and in the particular. His memory is overburdened with details, and he has no general plan.

It would be rash to formulate an iron rule of method, for there are those who thrive on a habit of inspired disorder; but for the average man it is good that he should apply business principles to his work. And for the orderly arrangement of topics a printed syllabus has been found invaluable. One of the lecturers on early constitutional history at Cambridge has been accustomed to furnish his class with two thirty-two page pamphlets, the first covering the ground to A.D. 1215 and the second from A.D. 1215 to A.D. 1485. These include a list of books recommended, a statement of the subject-matter of each lecture, and short paragraphs on points of special difficulty, with abundant references to the best sources of information. A lecturer on later constitutional history adopts a less ambitious plan, and confines himself to some twenty pages, but he also provides a list of books recommended and a scheme of each lecture.

Another feature of history-teaching in Cambridge is the series of weekly or fortnightly papers or essays set by each lecturer in connection with his class. These essays are not compulsory, but in a class of 45 or 50 members as many as 25 or 30 will write them. The lecturer looks over the essays beforehand, and then meets the writers privately, in groups of three or four, for criticism and discussion. Not many have the genius for this kind of oral teaching which is required to produce the best results, but at the worst it is valuable for purposes of revision, and it is not difficult to make it something more. Fresh problems may be introduced, and documents may be dealt with more thoroughly than is possible under the formal conditions of the lecture-room. The statutes of the Reformation Parliament, the history of the Dissolution of the Monasteries, the importance of the State Trials in the constitutional history of the 17th century, are subjects which cannot be adequately treated in lecture because the time available is not sufficient, but they can be made to serve for the conversation class. The history of the Star Chamber is generally misunderstood by the average student, and it is convenient to have an opportunity of revising it. A comparison between the political ideas of Pym and Shaftesbury, or of Strafford and Cromwell, though open to the charge of irrelevance, has been found to be stimulating. It is more difficult to justify a digression on literary style. But experience clearly shows that in most cases the time thus spent is spent to advantage. The system encourages wider interests, sounder knowledge, and a more chastened style of expression. And this is in spite of the fact that here the Cambridge teacher labours under a special disadvantage. Since history-lecturing is intercollegiate—and this is to be defended on almost every other ground—he is at close quarters with an alien folk who belong to other Colleges, and with them constitutional history is his only point of contact. His relations with these are pleasant enough, and he may make a few friends among them, but he does not acquire the intimate personal knowledge of the individual which is an important element in successful oral teaching. The criticism tends to be too polite, and it takes too long to establish the necessary moral ascendency.

English constitutional history for the Historical Tripos is treated in two academical years, and some 70 lectures are allowed to each half of the subject. But mention should also be made of a short course of 15 lectures on comparative constitutions, which deals with the structure of different modern forms of government and their manner of working. In this course the English constitution is treated first; but the order of treatment is logical rather than historical, and stress is laid on those features which suggest comparisons and contrasts with the institutions of other States, as for instance, the legal omnipotence of the British Parliament or the English form of Cabinet government as compared with foreign imitations of it. The constitution of the United States of America is studied next, as the type of the maturer form of federal government, and such points are emphasised as the checks imposed on the will of the numerical majority, the comparatively independent position of the Federal and State executives, the relation of the Federal judiciary to the political departments of government, the rights of individuals which are guaranteed by the Constitution, and the committee system of legislation. The more advanced students are also encouraged to grapple with such thorny questions as the true seat of American sovereignty and the legal aspect of secession. The more notable of the modern French constitutions are next compared; what is native and fundamental in them is distinguished from what is accidental or the result of conscious imitation; and the significance of recent developments is explained. Attention is also given to such problems as the anomalous position of the President as head of the Executive, elected and at the same time irresponsible; the modern working of the principle of 'separation of powers'; the effect of the 'group' system in weakening Parliamentary government; and the extent and character of French centralisation. The constitutions of the German Empire and Switzerland are also dealt with on the same scale; the rest only for purposes of illustration and comparison, and to show the drift of modern constitutional changes. For students who have already worked at English constitutional history this course has been found of considerable use.

THE TEACHING OF HISTORY IN
SCHOOLS—AIMS.

IN the teaching of History we are, we may assume, dis-
pensed from the need of asking a question obviously required
in the case of Mathematics or Classics, the question, namely,
whether we urge its claims on the ground of the value of the
subject for its own sake as information, or on the ground of
its worth as intellectual and moral discipline. The function of
the teacher of History in providing knowledge useful to the
learner is by me taken for granted: this essay deals with the
more strictly educational aims which may guide those who, in
teaching the subject, desire to keep before themselves definite
ends as the necessary basis of right methods.

Now a school subject, apart from its relation to the utilities
of life, may primarily be chosen for its aid in training intellectual faculty, *e.g.* Geometry, or taste, *e.g.* Literature or Drawing.
But there are broader ends still which may be applied as tests
in the estimate of educational values. Perhaps we may say
that a subject makes its strongest claims to a place in a school
course, when it not only increases knowledge and exercises
mental faculty, but when it stimulates interest in larger views of
life and action, and provides the continuance of that interest
when the initiative of the teacher is withdrawn. History does
all this. It has the merit that applications of its lessons are
always ready to hand: unlike Chemistry, it needs no laboratory,
unlike Geometry, its interest is never merely technical. It

shares with Literature and Philosophy the highest intellectual and moral attractiveness, in dealing with subject-matter of perennial concern to human life and motive.

It is necessary, next, to distinguish the elements of our intellectual faculty with which History has chiefly to do. We are all aware that our own earliest interest in History was nothing but an unconscious extension of our interest in story-telling. The most enduring historical acquisitions we have made are those early stories of the Old Testament, of Greece, Rome and England which came to each of us, originally, before History as a subject concerned us at all. The reason why they have thus survived lies in the fact that such stories appealed to our imagination, satisfied it, and stimulated it to dwell with pleasure on their repetition. This fitness of the story to the childish mind depended, no doubt, partly on its Old World simplicity, on its balance, perhaps on its striking literary form. But the essential factor in the appeal of narrative to the young is its quality of imaginative stimulus. History then begins by being, and ought always on certain sides of it to continue to be, an exercise of *constructive imagination.*

In the earliest stage of History teaching the aim is just this: to arouse the class to realise in mental picture the action, scene and character presented by the subject chosen: just as, in a much later stage, the same capacity for realising the emotions called into play by the great formative ideas of social organisation is essential to comprehending their force. The difference between a lesson that becomes knowledge, and one that does not, lies partly, at any rate, in the vividness of imagination which has been brought into activity in the course of it. Nor may we expect, in the case of younger scholars, that the learner will be able to bring this imaginative faculty to bear, unless the teacher directly arouses it. The book will not arouse it, such a book, I mean, as any class is able to use. Hence we touch at once upon the primary function of the History teacher in the elementary stages; he must *teach* and not merely hear a lesson. The latter may conduce to exercise of memory, but never of imagination. Voice, manner, fertility of illustration, unconscious emphasis, instinctive knowledge of the child's familiarity with action and with moral qualities, the constant testing of the ground, the imaginative insight into the subject dealt with—all these the teacher has and the book cannot have: these *make* the teacher. Thus we notice that the teacher's imagination forms the dominant factor here. Masters are apt to say that they cannot teach History to very young children : in that these have so little power of taking in facts that are outside their experience. It is meant, to put it into other words, that children have so little imagination. But the true reason is that the Master has so little; and that, again, means that he has not exercised it, and has not supplied it with proper, and with sufficient, material. For a ready yet truthful imagination demands fulness of material, much more than does a mere memory. For we need to play with our subject, to feel instinctively the analogies and the contrasts that it admits of, so to be able to express it in rapidly sketched pictures, with emphasis and proportion true to realities.

In preparing any lesson the teacher thus has more to do than to make sure of the actual facts with which it deals. He must seize the points which these may offer, or be made to offer, for clear and precise word-pictures. In the youngest classes, matter which does not readily lend itself to this treatment should be at once avoided as unsuitable. Characters, whose broad lines of good and bad qualities are easily recognisable, incidents of romantic sort—material which we find more frequently in the earlier stages of history—are naturally first chosen. But we should notice that all 'good' qualities do not appeal to the child : ascetic, contemplative, passive virtues make little impression. The instinct of the child's moral nature, as of his physical, is towards action. It is true that imagination is aroused by contrasts with daily experience, rather than by similarities, but this contrast must be sought in the surroundings and in the larger scale of the activity: not in the selection of types of life and conduct which are outside the range of a child's sympathies. The same is true of events. Unfamiliarity is the surest means of rousing interest, but the imagination will only be fruitfully exercised if the new matter is brought home by being put into some relation with what is already known. Without that, too great strain is placed upon the constructive faculty, and like a clumsy description in a book of travel the lesson fails to suggest any mental picture at all.

The teacher's imagination, then, must be alert. It must, in the next place, be restrained. The question arises in connection with stories avowedly unhistorical. We cannot possibly eliminate them from teaching. But the imagination is not to be let loose because we are no longer on the hard ground of fact. The teacher must stick to the myth. In treating the narrative of events the same restraint is needed, in omitting pictures or images which are out of all useful relation to the scholar's capacity. It is, for instance, of no avail to force imaginative conceptions of abstract ideas: feudalism, empire, autonomy, and the like.

Beginners are best relieved of any attempt to grasp social or political organisation. It is an utter mistake to 'start with the concrete,' in the sense in which some writers on historical method have advocated it. There is nothing which appeals to the imagination in the 'policeman,' the 'juryman,' the 'magistrate,' or the 'mayor' (*quâ* mayor); and to try to rise from such 'concrete instances' to conceptions of 'Order,' 'Government,' 'Law' and 'Kingship' is perfectly futile. A teacher may in this manner get in a certain amount of useful information, but it will prove uninteresting, and it is therefore premature. The teacher, knowing the imaginative value to himself of these outward emblems of national polity, may fancy that he can stimulate his class to an equal interest. But he must remember that his imaginative faculty, with its wide resources of fact, is no criterion of the strength of that of his scholars, and that, to be a trustworthy guide, it must be kept in constant restraint during a lesson. In reality *ideas* are unsuited for teaching purposes in case of the very young. 'The King' is abstract : William I. is concrete: the first will fail as an exercise of imagination, the other will succeed. 'Law' as an abstract authority is unintelligible to children, who will however readily understand the Forest Law of the Conqueror.

It will be asked at this point: "How far does this method of teaching aim at laying the foundations of subsequent study of the subject?" The reply is, that the truest preparation for future progress does not consist in imparting a body of knowledge, which will save time at a later stage, but in inspiring a taste, and in training the necessary intellectual faculty, for further acquisition. The actual retention of a number of facts and dates is, no doubt, usefully secured as early as possible. But this is only a minor service, when done. It will be of far greater importance to have stimulated interest in the historic past, and to have developed a power of seeing its incidents in clear-cut mental pictures.

The distinction between a logical and a psychological method of treating a subject of instruction is not without special helpfulness in considering methods of History teaching. Where a subject lends itself to so much variety of approach, we may fairly adopt the avenue which leads straight to the learner's interest. The teacher then is not concerned with the logical order of the material, but with its affinity to the child-mind. At this stage relative importance of historical subject-matter for teaching purposes is determined by the appeal it makes to the child's imagination, not by intrinsic value.

In a broad sense Patriotism rests partly on carefully-restrained appeals to imagination ; and I know of no reason why this may not form a definite end of the teaching of History almost from the beginning. The love of country and pride in it may be allowed to precede the sense of duty to one's country. Citizenship—one concrete side of Patriotism—is a conception to be slowly won at a much later period. But the germs of patriotic feeling must be planted by the agency of the imaginative faculty, and indeed it can never be wholly independent of it.

It will follow from what has been urged so far that the most profitable material for the first stages of History teaching will be found in primitive, rather than in modern, periods. In its appeal to children, a childlike age of humanity is more successful than its complex manhood. Hence the supreme interest of the stories of the Old Testament, of early Greece and Rome. The simplicity of ideas, the predominance of the elementary moral qualities, the importance of the individual, all render the pictures of early History intelligible to the young. There are, of course, admirable instances in our own History. But the old practice of teaching ancient story rather than modern had its basis in sound educational theory.

The second chief function in the disciplinary use of History is that of introducing the growing mind to reflection upon cause and effect in human affairs : in other words, that of training the *reasoning faculty*. It is one of the aims of teaching in all subjects to substitute in the growing mind rational associations of ideas for arbitrary ones. That William I. succeeded Harold II. may be remembered by arbitrary association, if it is a matter of mere verbal memory of names and dates : by rational association, the actual fact is seen to be the result of a number of antecedents which can be taught and grasped. The importance to memory of such higher associations needs not to be pointed out. This may help the Master to determine the method of teaching facts and dates : if he can, let the relation of cause and effect be first understood, then the sequence of events, being now *necessary*, is remembered without effort.

The capacity for looking for, and estimating, the right sequence of events can be trained from an early age : cruelty induces revenge, bad rule, rebellion. Naturally the power comes into play when a fuller knowledge of facts has been acquired. But the Master can help his class in marking out the clear line of development in his subject and in freeing the main thread of causation from episodes and side issues; obscure and unrelated connections will be discarded, and the class taught to follow out the successive links in the chain. The break up of the Athenian Empire or the revolt of the American Colonies afford obvious examples of matter suitable for the specific teaching of cause and effect in affairs. Moral causation will not less easily be inculcated. The rigid self-discipline of the Spartan State and its consequences in the place of Lacedaemon in Greece, contrasted with the degeneracy of the Persian monarchy and its collapse. So too the story of Ethelred, or of Richard II., or of France in the 18th century exhibit instances of the effects of moral decline.

The comparative method, which I would advocate even from the beginning, will enable a teacher to enforce these lessons by reference to analogies drawn from other histories. The Jews, the Greeks, the Romans and the English are available for the purpose. The influence of *character* in causation ; the inevitable march of revolution ; the forces working for national decline ; the effects of geography on national life, of commerce upon empire—every one of these central phenomena of History can only be securely taught when reasoning from one country to another is guided and filled out by the teacher. This is in no sense digression : it is utilising History as the finest instrument for reasoning upon human action.

There is another aspect in which the reasoning faculty of a class may be stimulated and exercised by the judicious History Master. I am referring to the mental discipline afforded by the critical method : the estimate of the value of historical evidence. This involves reasoning on the general probability of *facts* as recorded, and on the available knowledge or presumable bias on the part of the historian.

To illustrate how far from difficult such an introduction to criticism in reality is, it may be worth while to instance an example which the writer has known to be worked out with a class of boys of 16 years old: Shakespeare's *Henry VI.*, in relation to the life of Richard, Duke of Gloucester. It forms an easy and very effective study in the laws of historical credibility. The examination turns on (*a*) probability of facts, (*b*) bias of narrator; the entire apparatus of criticism lies in small compass and is easily accessible.

In the same way the value of the evidence of Herodotus or of Livy; the allowance to be made for bias in Tacitus, in a modern American historian, or Mr Carlyle: all this is in upper Forms perfectly appropriate material for the training of the reasoning faculty. It is not of least importance that such critical enquiry introduces the young scholar to the habit—as difficult as it is valuable—of handling books with freedom and self-reliance.

The third element of intellectual capacity which History brings into exercise is that of *Judgment*. The word is used rather loosely, but it is one for which we cannot well find a substitute. By 'practical judgment' I mean the faculty of estimating action (1) as regards the adjustment of means to ends, and (2) as regards its rightness in the moral sphere. The first is insight into the action of a man, or of a body of men, or of the State as a whole, judging it in respect of its wisdom, skill, genius, as manifested in the choice and pursuit of certain ends. The second is the moral estimate of this action: or, as we usually speak of it under this aspect, Conduct.

This quality of practical judgment here indicated is one which History pre-eminently cultivates. The great English masters of history, Arnold, Stubbs, Gardiner, have insisted on the virtue which goes forth from the earnest study of their subject in respect of the development of this capacity.

History is the record of the action of men, guiding, and guided by, the operation of ideas more or less imperfectly grasped. But civilised men and States are always aiming at some object, which they have set before themselves, worthy or unworthy, avowed or secret. The study of History teaches us to disentangle these aims, to discern how they came to be sought and what means were devised to attain them. Now, as all life, individual or corporate, is the exhibition of this same effort at devising aims and at adjusting means to securing them, we are, in historical enquiry, on familiar ground. It is not here suggested that historical study serves peculiarly as training in judgment in the private or individual capacities of life. But the citizenship of a self-governing State demands the constant exercise of that judgment which History can best inform and enlighten. For by it we consider the action of individuals— their skill, motives and ends ; by it we estimate the ideals and the policy of nations. The career of Pericles, of Caesar, of Charlemagne, wisely taught, will form admirable training in political judgment ; and, though the problem is more complex, so will the imperial policy of Athens, of Spain, or of England. Let it be understood that the work of the Master is not to frame and impart conclusions of his own, but to lead his class to distinguish such factors as are of crucial weight, and to estimate the limits within which judgments may be reasonably formed. The History lesson, then, is not only a series of mental pictures, not only a reasoned ordering of causes and results, but an attempt to view men and policies as complete wholes, with a view to a tentative verdict upon the skill and the moral sincerity which they exhibit. It is sometimes necessary, in such teaching, to discern between a man and his cause, to judge so carefully that our verdict is in favour of the one, but against the other: approving Demosthenes, but doubtful of his policy ; distrustful of Charles, but cherishing much that was unluckily identified with him.

History read in this spirit may, as nothing else can, help to correct some inevitable tendencies of maturer youth: such as the habit of forming hard, uncompromising opinions. Judgment will imply charity and caution in riding pre-conceptions too hard. It will teach us to see something of the intangible forces that overrule personal preferences and hinder the direct application of principles sincerely held.   The teacher will point out how good men, if weak, may do greater harm than worse men who are strong; how bad motives may somehow end in results which are for the welfare of the many.   From him should proceed the lesson that sweeping denunciations and wide moral generalisations are often false, and may merely cover up indolence in the search for truth, or the partiality of sectarian zeal.   On such judgment as this, fortified by resources of clearly-reasoned facts, the true patriotic emotion may be based.   To teach Citizenship as Herbert Spencer would have us do, turning our history lessons into descriptive sociology, will, we may confidently assume, prove a dismal failure.   The way to the higher sense of patriotic duty does not lie through the enumeration and analysis of the specific forms which the duties of citizenship may take in actual life.   Patriotism is a double obligation, a local and an imperial duty, and the stimulus to it must be first sought in the nobler emotions which revolve round inherited responsibilities.

Throughout the school course in History, these would seem to be the special ends to be kept in view by a Master who desires to make of his subject a truly effective factor in intellectual development: the stimulation and exercise of imagination, reasoning, judgment, and the patriotic sense.

THE TEACHING OF HISTORY IN SCHOOLS—PRACTICE.

HISTORY has obtained in English Schools within recent years a new importance. It no longer ranks amongst the voluntary 'extras' in the School curriculum. More time is given to its study; it is recognised as having other functions in Education besides that of stocking the memory with useful information, and many Schools possess at least one Master who has had some Historical training at the University.

Its place in Education however, though reconsidered, is not yet settled. At present there is no unanimity amongst the Theorists or the Teachers. There is no agreement as to what the aims in the teaching of History should be, or as to what History in Schools can or cannot do. Divergence of aim is partly responsible for the differences in the time allotted to History (varying from $\frac{3}{4}$ of an hour a week in some Schools to five hours in the Modern and three in the Classical side at others), and also for the astonishing diversity in the methods employed in the Teaching. Every School is a law unto itself; and in most Schools every master may teach History in the way which seems to him to be best—or easiest. Such independence and variety has its advantages, and is consistent with the principles of English education. But as a consequence it is impossible for a writer on the Teaching of History to detail English methods as he would those of the Germans. The present writer therefore does not propose to give a complete account of History Teaching in Schools—that at present is impossible—nor to draw up elaborate schemes or dictate Methods. All he can do is to note deficiencies, to point out difficulties which he himself has met with, and to make suggestions as a result of his own experience and the experience of others.

First of all something must be said with regard to the general organization of History Teaching.

A contrast might easily be drawn between the completeness of the German system and the incomplete arrangements of most English Schools. At present, however, the German system cannot be naturalised in England. At most, if not all, Schools the time allotted to History is insufficient; in some it is too absurdly inadequate to permit even important periods to be covered twice, which is one characteristic of the German system. Moreover, the lack of trained teachers makes the study of General History with the same elaborateness as in Germany quite impossible, and attempts made are apt to lead to a boy being crammed with masses of unconnected facts and names, or to an unintelligent reading of some universal History. And things being as they are, the present writer is not at all sure that in the higher forms, 'if a choice, from lack of time, has to be made, a detailed knowledge of one Period is not more valuable than a very slight acquaintance with a good many.

But if under existing circumstances a big measure of reform is impossible, many amendments may at least be carried out. In some schools History is made subservient to Classics, and only Ancient History is taught in the top divisions; at others Ancient History is ignored in the Sixth Form. In some schools long and important Periods are left untouched: of nearly all it would be true to say that their teaching of Modern History is too insular, and ignores foreign countries. As a consequence, some boys do not possess even an acquaintance in dates with the Period which witnessed the decline of the Roman Empire; and yet this is the Period which the greatest of English historians has made his own. Other boys are without any adequate or connected knowledge of the History of their own country, or of its Empire. Again, nearly all boys are extraordinarily ignorant of Foreign History; and that ignorance results in narrowness of view, and in an insular contempt of other nations which familiarity with their History would alone dispel.

But it is easy to point out deficiencies; it is a harder task to suggest remedies. Something may be done by a rearrangement of the Periods studied; something to remedy gross ignorance by a book of dates; History must cease to be regarded as the handmaid of Classics; most important of all, more time must be given to History, and more teachers.

So much may be said as to organisation; and now some suggestions may be made as to the use of what may be termed the instruments in History Teaching—the Text-books, Illustrations, Atlases. On one point teachers are agreed; Text-books, except in teaching very small boys, are indispensable. The necessary facts—the Grammar—of History must be learnt by reading and not by hearing; it is the business of the book to narrate, of the teacher to illustrate, explain, supplement. For English and for Ancient History there is an ever-increasing supply of Text-books for both small and big boys. For European History, it is harder to find suitable Text-books; Freeman's *General Sketch* gives the elementary facts for young boys, and for more advanced students there are such books as Lodge's *Modern Europe*, the Periods of European History published by Messrs Rivington, and Macmillan's Foreign Statesmen Series. But good intermediate Text-books are still needed, though Longmans' Epoch Series is useful for special periods.

In some schools, the younger boys are still the victims of abridgements; and we are not yet free from the traditional

A. 6

methods of those who abridge with the result that History, as a French writer has put it, appears as a series of wars, treaties, reforms, revolutions, differing only in the names of the peoples, sovereigns, fields of battle, and in the figures giving the year.

To come to another subject—the part that illustrations should play in the Teaching of History. It is being more and more recognised that in education boys should learn, not only by reading and hearing, but also by observation. And in History especially a great deal can be taught by sight. The younger boys will receive a more definite, clear, and lasting impression from what they see, than either from what they read or from what they hear; with all boys illustrations will make History more real, and consequently more interesting; and illustrations are not without their value in stimulating the imagination, and in making more keen the boy's power of observation.

Moreover, of recent years a great deal has been done to supply illustrations. Some Text-books are filled with admirably chosen ones. Photographs of buildings, coins, engravings, can be had in plenty. Photographs of portraits are easily procurable, and though boys cannot judge character from them, yet a good portrait will enable them to realise that historical personages were real flesh and blood, and not remote beings ticketed with dates. The Germans, again, have published a collection of coloured pictures, in which striking events in History are reproduced with the most scrupulous fidelity. There is no difficulty in getting or making lantern-slides; some firms have very complete and elaborate collections; and the present writer has found no difficulty in getting leave from publishers to make slides from pictures in books. The lantern can best illustrate campaigns, whether ancient or modern, on sea or on land, whether they be those of Hannibal or Nelson. By its means the social life of a past epoch can most easily be realised. A series of pictures of the Roman Wall for instance will give a boy some notion of the greatness of the Roman

Empire, and form an admirable introduction to its history. Slides showing Pompeii (as it was and as it is), Pompeian shops, the games of the circus, displays in the amphitheatre as illustrated by frescoes, reliefs, and coins, will give a boy some conception of its social life. To take but one other example of a different kind. The British Museum authorities have just published a most interesting and well-chosen series of facsimiles of letters at a very moderate price. Some fiery notes of Henry VIII. written in the margin of a document of Latimer's, and contemning his attack upon Purgatory, a page from Edward VI.'s diary about the conversion of his sister Mary, a letter of Mary Stuart to Elizabeth complaining of the rigour of her imprisonment, a document signed by the English commanders after the defeat of the Armada, declaring that they would follow and pursue the enemy until they had left our shores, a page from the log of Ralegh's ship on his last voyage, it is such letters as these that excite in a boy that personal interest in historical characters without which History loses for the young its reality and its charm. Moreover it is by examining such letters that a boy may make his first approach to original documents, and learn that it is from thousands of manuscripts such as these that the historian must largely form his judgment of the men and events of a past age[1].

An Atlas of Historical Geography is of course an indispensable instrument in the teaching of History; indeed its necessity is so obvious, and by this time so generally

[1] The Art for Schools Association, Messrs Mansell & Co. of Oxford Street, and Messrs Spooner of the Strand have very large collections of photographs of buildings, pictures, portraits; Messrs Newton & Co. and Messrs Philip & Son, both of Fleet Street, have varied series of lantern-slides, including slides from such books as the illustrated edition of Green's *Short History*, and Gardiner's *Students' History*; specimens of some of the illustrations used abroad may be seen in the Museum of the Teachers' Guild of Gower Street, W.C. Schreiber's *Atlas of Classical Antiquities* for Ancient History, and Lavisse's *Album Historique* (4 volumes—Colin et Cie.) for Mediæval and Modern History are excellent.

recognised, that it is superfluous to prove it. For English History, Gardiner's Atlas is excellent and quite adequate for most boys, and it does not neglect foreign countries; but there is room for another which should contain more details and more Maps. In European History, there is the Oxford Historical Atlas, now in course of publication, which I have found most useful in teaching older boys. For Ancient History, Murray's new series of Maps is quite admirable. Teachers will, of course, find the elaborately detailed maps published in Germany most useful for themselves.

Something must now be said of the methods of teaching. Foreigners tell us that in education, as in all else, we have no care for method. We certainly have not been drilled into the rigid and possibly mechanical system prescribed for the Continental Teacher. We are in favour of liberty and independence in teaching, and consequently there is every variety of method, both good and bad. That variety, even if it is undesirable, is unavoidable. The methods employed in teaching must largely depend upon the time allotted to History, and upon the knowledge, the character, and the experience of the particular teacher.

In treating of method, it is necessary to make some division of the boys according to their ages. Of teaching in the preparatory stages—before a boy comes to a Public School—the present writer, having no practical experience, proposes to say nothing.

With regard to Public Schools, boys in the Lower Forms must learn the main facts in the chief periods, and provided that the dates are supplied in reasonable quantities a boy from 13 to 15 has no very special horror of them; he prefers the facts to be put in a concise and definite form; and he can learn them with less difficulty then than at any later period of his existence. For the learning of dates the writer has no new suggestion; some teachers exercise their ingenuity in making rhymes and puzzles, and provided that they are not so ingenious as to confuse, and yet ingenious enough to please the boys, they may be of use. For the supply of dates some have suggested a short book of a few pages, containing the chief dates, names and facts of History to be learnt like a Grammar, and to be in use throughout a school. Others—and probably this is better— have a more graduated list, containing a list of dates for the younger boys: for those higher up the original dates in big type, supplemented by others in smaller type; for those at the top a still larger list. Even an acquaintance merely in dates with great events and great men is better than complete ignorance. Boys when they are young should also possess some time-chart of the World's History to enable them to measure the periods of time covered, the comparative length of Ancient, Mediaeval and Modern History, and to realise even vaguely the "Unity of History." The History of each country or people in teaching the younger boys must be treated separately, and isolated; but as a consequence boys fail, for instance, to connect in time the History of Greece and Rome, or events in English History with great events abroad. They altogether fail to appreciate the length of the early periods in the world's history[1].

In the actual teaching, most would agree that the periods with boys in the Lower Forms should be done quickly, the great object being to cover the chief epochs in outline; that the ordinary teaching must consist in explaining and supple-menting the text-book; that *vivâ voce* questions should be asked, if not so systematically as in Germany, at all events with great frequency and with some method. With regard to written questions, a number of short questions on the text-book involving written answers of three or four lines may help a boy to read a book intelligently, and shorter

[1] A recent writer has suggested a 'line of time' which each boy can make for himself, the scale being two inches to 500 years, and the periods, events, and dates can be filled in at discretion. It will please a boy's ingenuity to make such a line and to place a date 'in scale' accurately.

questions with almost monosyllabic answers may teach him accuracy. The American 'recitation' might be of great value in teaching a boy not only History, but also how to connect his ideas and give a clear narrative when he is standing on his legs. A great deal may be done by black-board illustration[1].

At the same time it must be remembered that boys at that age are learning grammar in Latin, Greek, French ; their History should stimulate and interest as well as inform. It does not interest lower boys to show how the control of the purse-strings affected the power of the House of Commons, or to follow closely the relations between the Stuarts and their Parliaments. But they are keenly interested in fighting, they like to know how battles were lost and won, they love to make maps and plans. They are hero-worshippers and like biography. Lectures should be given occasionally dealing in detail with particular wars or biographies. A life of Hannibal if they are doing Roman History, of Ralegh if they are studying Elizabeth's reign, the history of the long bow and its victories for the earlier wars with France, of the three-decker for the later wars, will be a refreshing break from lists of dates and kings, wars and treaties, and will teach them as much history.

In the higher forms of schools (including roughly boys from 16 to 19) the teaching of History changes its character. It is in these forms that boys learn that History is not a fortui-tous concourse of facts and events but must be studied in connexion with cause and effect, and that they must use their reasoning powers as well as their memory in order to understand it. From this time the oral teaching becomes of more importance than the text-book. After all the best of text-books will by itself teach but little History. A boy might know his text-book by heart, and yet have but a small acquaintance with the period which the book is supposed to cover. It is the teacher— before a boy can read much for himself—who must generalise

[1] Mr Somervell has given some ingenious examples of this method of teaching in a book called *Teaching and Organisation.*

from and analyse facts; who must give his judgment on men and events; who must explain causes and estimate effects; and who must stimulate and give the real guidance. The oral teaching should now begin to take the form of a lecture; the text-book need not be followed, and the History should be taught by subjects.

The boy must learn how to take notes on Lectures. In beginning a boy is apt to put down the unessential or to leave out what is necessary; a virtuous boy is apt to measure his virtue by the number of pages covered, and to spread over 10 pages what he might easily have compressed into 3; if he is very virtuous he may follow the example of the Cambridge young lady in whose note-book appeared the opening words of the lecturer, "Last time I began by saying." But a boy soon learns to have an eye for the chief points, will not waste words, will use abbreviations, will not forget quotations or illustrations, and will know what to neglect. In lecturing on English History to large classes at the top of the school, the present writer has found it a great advantage to prepare a printed Syllabus for circulation amongst the boys which contains the outline of the Lecture and the chief facts, tables of dates and genealogies, quotations from contemporary writers and from modern historians, short lists of books, and blank pages for the boy to take notes. Such a syllabus saves the Lecturer much dictation and the boys much mechanical note-taking, and is of service for reference, whilst the boys appreciate the quotations, and the blank pages enable them to take notes quickly without the necessity of a note-book[1].

Though, however, the teaching should be mainly by lecturing it should not be wholly so. *Vivâ voce* questions must be asked continually, to see whether the boys have understood, remembered, attended, and in order that they may themselves suggest where possible the causes or results of a particular

[1] Copies of these Syllabuses may be obtained from Messrs Spottiswoode and Co., Eton College.

event or policy; and even the dignity of a Sixth Form boy may be occasionally startled by a question of a very elementary or very recondite nature. Numerous explanations, digressions, illustrations may prevent note-taking becoming mechanical; and more especially the boy should write answers to questions.

It is now, if not before, that the questions set not only test a boy's knowledge but his ability, not only his facts and dates but his capacity to use them, argue from them, interpret them. It is extraordinary how difficult some boys at first find it to answer questions which demand the use of their reason as well as their memory. They will for instance give a good account of the Civil War with many details; but any question which involves the use and not a mere statement of the facts makes them helpless. They can, as they express it, "write out" a reign or a life, but any question asking what claims a man has to be considered a great Statesman or a great General will produce either great quantities of fluent nonsense or an alarming mass of very solid narrative. A boy should be able to write an answer in a limited time in which facts should be used to illustrate points or support arguments, which should keep to the question and be well arranged, and which should be withal forcibly and brightly expressed. That is the ideal; it would be absurd of course to say that all or even most boys attain to it. Some boys cannot pick out easily what they want from a heap of material; others find it difficult to keep to the point, and will sometimes write an answer which has but a remote connexion with the question, or will fly off at a tangent half-way through the answer. Some will use slang when they try to be forcible, and scatter epithets with no discretion when they wish to write well; the answers of others never succeed in escaping the charge of dulness. But all boys will improve with practice, and this practice affords a most valuable training.

One or two other points may be noticed. Boys in the higher forms might do historical essays, and for these they should be encouraged to read larger books, the subjects of course being selected with a view to interest, and so set as to allow of some originality of treatment. Moreover they should be introduced to the works of the great historians; in the middle forms this can best be done by reading out passages— a scene from Froude, a description from Macaulay, a chapter of some biography will give boys a prospect of the future delights of History; in the higher forms the boys should be urged to read for themselves. Some attempt ought to be made to take in detail some Period either in Ancient or English History, tracing not only its political but also the economic, constitutional, social and literary History. The Oxford and Cambridge Certificate Examination requires a Period to be thus studied. For at least one term in the year European History should be studied, and clever boys take to Political Science without any difficulty.

It is easy enough, however, to make suggestions; it is impossible to adopt them unless more time is devoted in most schools to History, and, what is equally important, allowed to the teacher for preparation. In the sixth form for instance of most public schools where from one to one and a half hours in a week is devoted to History, it is difficult to find time to do more than ask short questions from the text-book, to Lecture and set very occasionally a paper; moreover if the boys are specialists in classics they have little opportunity for historical reading, and no time to do essays. At some schools the difficulty of time is partly solved in the higher forms by making History an optional subject amongst many others, one of which must be taken, and boys who are interested in History can choose it as their subject.

Finally something may be said of the Specialists, of boys, who though they may not have given up classics are reading for scholarships, or have settled to read History at the Universities, and so in their last year make History their first subject. With the latter class, the teacher has a free hand; he is not limited by examinations, and his only object is to teach them to read history intelligently and to give them a solid foundation to build upon later. An attempt may be made to give these boys a clear outline of English History and if possible of some foreign period ; they should read "general" books, the works of such writers as Bagehot, Dicey, Seeley, Maine ; they should also write more elaborate essays than the ordinary boy has time to do ; and above all, they should be carefully taught the proper methods of Historical study, so that they may not— as so many do—lose time when they reach the University. But a promising boy, at that age, if too young to form judgments, will at any rate possess prejudices. He will take interest in, and show enthusiasm for, particular periods or particular men. He should be encouraged to read as much and as deeply as possible on a subject which interests him, and may be introduced to the original authorities. Happy indeed is the teacher who has many such boys. There can be no more delightful task than stimulating and directing the enthusiasm of a youthful historian.

A word may be said in conclusion as to History Scholarships. It is well to remember that the Examinations at Oxford and Cambridge differ in their demands, and that the character and interests of a boy must largely determine for which University he should be a candidate. Cambridge examinations demand a wide knowledge ; at one college there are papers on the World's history, on the whole of English History, on the History of Political Government, and on a foreign period, and in each paper eight out of the twelve questions have to be answered. The questions present no great difficulty if the facts are familiar. At Oxford on the other hand it is better to possess a detailed knowledge of one period than a superficial acquaintance with a great many; only five or six out of twelve questions need be answered, but they necessitate more than a text-book acquaintance with a subject ; great stress is laid on the general papers in which questions are set on all subjects, from Art to Political Economy, and on the essay ; and a boy may be helped materially by his classics. 'Spes non res' is the Oxford motto, and the answers are judged, perhaps in a greater degree than at Cambridge, not only by the knowledge displayed, but by their arrangement and arguments, their style and attractiveness.

But the number of pages allotted to this Chapter is already exceeded. The claims of History are still matter of debate, but the present writer has no doubt that History will fill a larger place in education in the future than it does now. For History in schools may not only provide boys with information "which is part of the apparatus of a cultivated life," but should do something to stimulate the imagination of the young, to develop the reason of those who are older, possibly to train the judgment of a few in the Highest Forms. It may extend the mental horizon of all. It may and should provoke patriotism and enthusiasm; it should help to train the Citizen or the Statesman ; its study should lead to right feeling and to right thinking. Yet a teacher who has all or some of these aims will frequently be dissatisfied with himself and his methods, and will be conscious more often of failure than of success. But that is the lot of all who teach. Some satisfaction may be obtained if one succeeds in preparing a boy to read History for himself and to appreciate its lessons in after-life.

THE TEACHING OF HISTORY
IN AMERICA.

To give anything like a complete account of the historical teaching in American universities would be an exceedingly difficult, if not impossible, undertaking. For the individualism which characterises the political and economic life of the United States marks also their educational activity; and it has produced a bewildering congeries of institutions, all exercising the power of conferring academic degrees, but exhibiting in their standards an incomparably wider diversity than can be found in any of the countries of Europe. It is true that some even of the smallest of these institutions are doing excellent work. They often provide opportunities for a higher culture to "constituencies" which, from want of means, inadequate previous education or religious prejudice, would be kept away from the greater universities. In judging of them it is not always possible to separate provincial ignorance from local patriotism or sectarian jealousy from self-denying zeal. Still this state of things makes it peculiarly hard to generalize. "Courses of instruction," which on paper look very much alike, may in actual practice be separated by the whole gamut of possible difference,—at the one end a quite Teutonic *Gründlichkeit*, at the other the unintelligent reproduction of ill-chosen text-books. And, if one surveys the whole field of American education, these standards will be found to shade into one another by insensible gradations. This helps to explain what at first seems so curious to the European scholar who joins the staff of a famous American university: the absence of sharp lines of demarcation, and the kindly tolerance which his colleagues display towards institutions which he is inclined to dismiss with contempt. Their attitude has this further justification, that the tendency is now quite distinctly in the direction of improvement all round. Every year more and more of those men, who after graduating at a small institution have benefited by a period of further study at one of the greater centres of learning, are returning to teach in their old colleges with new scientific aspirations and new criteria of excellence. The process of levelling-up has grave obstacles to overcome, but it is making way.

The other difficulty in the way of generalisation is the remarkable variety in the forms of academic organisation to be found even among institutions of the first rank. The foreign observer is not only perplexed by such differences of custom and nomenclature as inevitably grow up in course of time, such for instance as may be found between Oxford and Cambridge; he is struck by the juxtaposition of terms which seem to belong to different national systems,—by the way, for instance, in which "freshmen" and "bachelors" and "marks" jostle against "Ph.D's" and "Seminaries," and even "Semesters" and "Docents." The clue to the maze is furnished by American college history. All the older American universities were originally colleges of the English type. I imagine that a traveller last century would have found little noticeable difference between the studies and modes of life in Emmanuel College, Cambridge, and in her great daughter, Harvard College, in Massachusetts. But when, soon after the great war was over in 1815, America was visited by the stirrings of new intellectual interests, it was to Germany that her young scholars all turned for instruction and inspiration. They went to Göttingen and Heidelberg, and returned with German conceptions of what a "University" should mean. The result was an attempt, in more than one instance, to place on top of the old-fashioned college of English type, a professorial university of the German pattern. The movement was perhaps premature at the time; but it was revived and carried much further when the second great wave of enthusiasm for the higher learning broke over America in the years that immediately followed 1870. And now the matter of university organisation is no longer a subject chiefly of theoretic interest to a few isolated scholars. The development of the country in population, wealth, social complexity and intellectual needs has brought "the faculty" of every considerable institution face to face with the two fundamental problems of academic policy. These are, in the first place, how to construct a curriculum for the ordinary student which shall combine scope for individual powers, and regard for the needs of the modern world with the claims of literary culture; and, secondly, how to reconcile the business of instruction in what is already known with the salutary impulse towards further investigation. Thanks partly to the mechanical genius of the American people, which makes all questions of method so exceedingly—one is sometimes inclined to think, excessively—interesting to them, these two problems are now being confronted with a pretty clear consciousness of their importance and of their interconnection. Ultimately, no doubt, a definite type of American university will be arrived at, appropriate to a modern industrial society. Meanwhile, the American college is in the experimental stage; and no one set of requirements for degrees, no one line of demarcation between "university" and "college," or between graduate and undergraduate studies, can be regarded as more obviously likely to prevail than any other of the half-dozen other experiments which are being tried elsewhere.

In spite of all these diversities, however, there are still a certain number of the larger features of academic life which are common to all the greater universities; and these I shall now attempt to set forth. I shall naturally enough have Harvard mainly in my mind as I go along; but although that oldest of American colleges has some marked peculiarities of its own, a word of caution here and there may suffice to prevent any serious misapprehension.

The most striking feature in the educational system of the American university is, I am inclined to think, the prominence of the "course." A "course" consists, in most places, of two or three hours of instruction per week, given most commonly by means of lectures, and running right through the academic year, together with prescribed reading and mid-year and final yearly examinations upon both reading and lectures. The same amount of work extending over only half the year,—the academic year is commonly divided into halves,—constitutes a "half-course"; and the like designation is sometimes given to half the amount of work spread over the whole year. In Harvard the student has an almost complete "freedom of election" among the hundreds of courses offered to him; and he receives his bachelor's degree on passing in a fixed number of courses; so that it is theoretically possible for him to make the most incongruous combinations. But the inevitable limitations of the time-table impose some restrictions; and, besides, undergraduates are very gregarious. The association for administrative purposes of the teachers of cognate subjects in "Divisions" and "Departments" (*e.g.* the Division of History and Political Science, which includes the Departments of History and Political Economy), would of itself suggest to the undergraduate that certain subjects are akin. There tends, therefore, to grow up a certain loose grouping of the students around the subjects which mainly attract their attention; approaching, though at a great distance, to the state of affairs produced at Oxford and Cambridge by the Schools and Triposes. At most other American universities there is far less freedom of selection among individual courses: the student has either to choose between a certain number of combinations of subjects, and with each subject take certain allotted courses, or, in very old-fashioned places, he pursues a common curriculum, with more or less recognition of the method of alternatives. But however large or small "the elective element" may be, the "course" is coming to be the real unit of work and examination. For the bachelor's degree there is nowhere, so far as I know, any examination covering the whole of a couple of years' work, like those for the Oxford Honour Schools or the Cambridge Triposes. It is the universal practice for the "instructor" "giving" a "course" himself to conduct the examination or examinations attached to it; this is, perhaps, inevitable with so wide a range of "electives." When the number in a class is large, the instructor is commonly enabled to appoint one or more assistants to help him with the reading of the papers; but there is no official position comparable to that of an "examiner" in an English university. The degree is conferred on the basis of the annual "returns" which the instructors give in to the university "office." Owing to the absence of outside examiners, and of any binding definition of what a course shall include, and also to the power of an instructor to modify his course year by year, the examination is not so much on a subject at large as upon the particular course in the way in which it was conducted in a particular year. However naturally some topic fell within the scope of a course, a student would usually feel aggrieved if he were asked some question upon it which had not been dealt with by the lectures or by "reading" definitely recommended.

What has been said of the prominence of the "course" will already have suggested the absence of any such tutorial system as has been elaborated at Oxford or as is beginning to make its appearance at Cambridge. There is no officer whose duty it is to supervise the whole of a student's work for a couple of years; to so guide his reading and assign such topics for weekly essays that he shall cover the whole of a certain large field (comparable in amount, perhaps, to eight courses) within the allotted time; and to hear and criticise these essays week by week both as to form and content. In an American University the student is left much more to himself, both for good and for ill. The instructors are very ready to advise him as to the selection of courses; in some universities there are official "advisers" for freshmen. Moreover there is a certain amount of supervision and individual help provided in connection with the several courses. In large elementary classes, numbering a couple of hundred students or more, it is usual to introduce frequent "tests," in the shape of "hour examinations," and to employ the services of a staff of "assistants" who hold "conferences," with such students as do badly on such occasions. It is the business of these assistants to assign definite bits of reading, and to see that the tasks are accomplished, after a fashion. In the case of the smaller classes, the instructor may confine himself to set lectures, and be content with the mid-year and final annual examinations as tests of application and intelligence. Or he may, and often does, assign pieces of "written work," commonly called "theses,"—perhaps as many as four in the course of the year, to each man. The quality of the performance, the amount of help given by the instructor, the thoroughness of the criticism, the extent of personal contact, differ with the nature of the course and the views and idiosyncrasies of the teacher. Speaking broadly, it may perhaps be said that the more intelligent and industrious students get about as much personal assistance, putting it all together, as they would in Oxford, while the lazy and stupid get a good deal less. The average American professor, it will be perceived, occupies a position midway between that of a German professor and that of an Oxford tutor. He sees more of the students than the former, less than the latter. But whatever help he may extend to his students, it is almost all in connection with the particular courses he is "giving" that year. Of course I am now speaking of official duty, and not of the offices of friendship.

The "course," conducted chiefly by way of lectures, being thus the pivot around which revolves the whole academic

A. 7

world, the character of the instruction it provides is of vital importance.   Naturally this varies with the subject.   In the elementary historical courses all that can be expected, or needed, is that the instructor should put before his hearers the salient points in the period, and should direct their attention to the "standard" writers who have dealt with it.   But a very noticeable feature in almost all the instruction above the most elementary is the stress laid on the use of the original "sources." This is not limited to the seminary work, to be described later : in many of the ordinary courses the instructors insist that students shall actually themselves consult some of the accessible printed collections of documents or contemporary narrative. From the universities the enthusiasm for "sources" is now spreading to the teachers of American and English History in the secondary schools; and I am not sure that "the new method" is not in danger of being pushed to extremes.   To put before a student a bit of contemporary narrative, with all its obvious bias and the unmistakeable colour of its time and place, and thus enable him, as it were, to watch history in the making, may give a new interest to the subject, and possibly awaken in a mind here and there the germs of a critical sense.   But as soon as "source books" have come to be produced, with the "portions" of contemporaries served up ready for immediate consumption, it has to be very good teaching indeed which induces the student to go further and look at the passages in their context.   No one who is acquainted with the Oxford History School will maintain that the use of the "Select Char-ters" has been an unmixed good.   Still, whatever dangers may lurk in "source books" for the *élite* of the students, they evidently supply the average man with a valuable supplement to the mere text-book.

The courses, it need hardly be said, range over the whole field of history.   My impression is that both Ancient History and General Mediaeval History attract relatively few students, and are represented by a relatively small number of teachers.   But

Mediaeval English History secures a surprisingly large amount of attention on its constitutional side. The continuity of English and American institutional development is taken for granted; and the great treatise of the Bishop of Oxford, supplemented by the writings of Professor Maitland and Mr Round, finds assiduous readers. Among courses on Modern History, those on America naturally attract most auditors. Their place in University life may be gathered from the following figures. In the year 1897–8 at Harvard, the general preliminary course on mediaeval and modern history, which most would-be students of history are obliged to take first, enrolled 439 students. Among the courses dealing with particular periods, that on American History since 1783 stood at the top in respect of numbers, with 210; European History since 1750 and American History before 1783 ran one another close with 171 and 169 respectively. Then came a great fall in numbers to English Constitutional History since 1760 with 107; and another great fall to Mediaeval English Constitutional History with 54, the History of the Eastern Question with 48, and England 1485—1688 with 44. In the ten other courses given that year the numbers ranged from 22 to 3. To show the large part played by American History, it must be added that among the courses given under the head of Political Economy was one on American Economic History which drew 94 students; and that in the Historical Seminary out of 25 students 17 worked at topics in American History. As a result alike of popular demand and of the awakening of a keen intellectual interest in the subject, the greater universities are finding it desirable to constitute two full professorships in American History, dividing the field most commonly at the year 1783. The whole movement is full of promise; it has found an organ in the *American Historical Review*; and the study of American History is evidently entering into the scientific stage. Already more than one popular notion as to the relations between the English of Britain and the English of

America in the 17th and 18th centuries is being abandoned to ill-informed Americanophils on the eastern side of the Atlantic.

The significance of the study of American History for the political life of the American people, especially at a time when it is assuming new responsibilities, is too obvious for comment. It is heightened by the fact that, side by side with the narrative courses, there are an increasing number of courses being established in the greater universities which are devoted to the comparative study of political institutions. At Harvard these are grouped together under the heading "Government," and are included within the Department of History; elsewhere they are differently designated and grouped; but the general result is much the same. They everywhere form a useful supplement to the "purely historical" courses; and in most cases they are quite concrete and "inductive" in their method. The more advanced courses,—such as that which at Harvard brings together a score of graduate and senior students, after an adequate preliminary preparation, to compare the working of the present political mechanism of England, France, Germany, and the United States,—constitute schools of Politics in the truest sense.

Next to the organization of the courses, the most striking feature in the American academic system is to be found in the Graduate Schools, which, under various names and varying organization, have grown up in all the larger universities. That at Harvard, for instance, numbers some 300 men; of whom about one-third are ordinary B.A.s of Harvard, and of the rest the great majority B.A.s of some other college of good standing (perhaps a fifth of them having also spent a year or two as undergraduates at Harvard, and added the Harvard degree to their earlier one). Out of the 300, perhaps every sixth or seventh pursues studies which lie chiefly in the realm of History and Political Science. After being accepted by the Committee on Admission from other colleges as "equal to a Harvard B.A." or having performed, if necessary, an assigned amount of work to bring them up to that standard, a student in the Graduate School may become a candidate for the degree of M.A., which is conferred only after passing satisfactorily in four courses of a certain grade. Or, if he can afford to stay two or three years, he may aspire to the degree of Ph.D. The doctorate is now coming to be the necessary avenue to any employment as an instructor in an American university; and it is aimed at by all the more ambitious members of the Graduate School. Accordingly the greater universities are all realising the need of jealously safeguarding its quality; and in the year 1898 it was secured in Harvard by 26 persons alone, of whom 3 were historians.

The conditions of the doctorate differ widely from place to place. In Harvard they are (1) a good preliminary education, (2) a fair knowledge of a certain general field, put together from a wide range of choice allowed by an official programme, (3) a more intimate knowledge of a special field, *e.g.* American Colonial History, or the Mediaeval Constitutional History of England, and (4) a dissertation based on the original investigation of some subject falling within the special field. More weight has come to be attached of late years to general culture, and to an intelligent appreciation of the significance of the larger movements of History: students allowed to give an almost exclusive attention to their special field and the preparation of their dissertation were already beginning to display the unfortunate results of excessive and premature specialisation. It is especially necessary to utilize the examination for the doctorate to secure a due correlation of studies, under a system of freedom of election and of examination for the B.A. degree on the single course.

The work of research carried on by the graduate student with a view to his doctoral dissertation finds its point of contact with the general academic life in the organization of the Seminary. Having chosen his subject the student is placed under the oversight of that one of the professors whose intellectual interests it most nearly touches, and from time to time takes counsel with him. The seminary, a fortnightly meeting, presided over by a professor, of graduate students (with occasional "seniors," *i.e.* 4th year undergraduates) all engaged in similar labours, is occupied with the reading or oral exposition of their "results." Its chief value lies in the salutary pressure which it brings to bear on the students to take stock once or twice a year of the progress of their investigations, to disentangle their conclusions and put them into shape, and so escape the danger of being overwhelmed by their accumulated data. A subsidiary purpose is to afford the other members of the seminary an object-lesson of what to do and what to avoid in the presentation of their material.

When the seminary was imported from Germany some twenty years ago, somewhat exaggerated expectations were entertained of its efficiency in stimulating intellectual activity. It was pictured as a group of ardent fellow-workers cooperatively engaged, though with a certain division of labour, in the pursuit of historic truth. In some places a particular room or even a suite of rooms was set apart for the seminary. Here they could hold their meetings, and here, with a special collection of sources and authorities at their elbow, they could pursue their labours apart from the vulgar mass of undergraduates. But several causes have rendered it difficult to carry out this ideal. It is not easy to find a subject for investigation which is capable of being broken up into a group of topics independent enough to satisfy the student's craving for a subject of his own, and connected enough to furnish a common interest. Even when this can be done one year, the mere fact that students are often engaged two or even three years upon their dissertation, would make it impossible to create a common interest every year. Accordingly, it must be confessed that most of the members of a seminary, having no special knowledge of the subject assigned to a particular afternoon, take only a languid interest in what is set before them, and contribute little in the way of discussion; while the professor who presides soon exhausts the generalities which occur to him. In consequence, the enthusiasm for "the seminary method" is evidently lessening; and in some quarters there are visible tendencies towards disintegration. There is the less need for regret, because the advanced courses, which are provided in much greater abundance in the larger American universities than in Germany, satisfy to some extent the same purpose as the *Seminar* was designed to accomplish, *i.e.* the promotion of original investigation. Still the introduction of the seminary marked a stage in the approach to the higher ideals of a university; and it still forms a useful part of the academic machinery.

The conditions of the doctorate, if they can be maintained,—and there seems no reason for alarm in this regard, so far as the greater institutions are concerned—provide a very effective stimulus towards research. But a certain influence in the same direction has already been exercised,—and this influence will probably grow,—by the markedly hierarchical organization of the teaching body. A graduate student of distinct ability, even before he has secured his Ph.D., can usually add considerably to his income and gain valuable experience, by acting for a year or so as "assistant" in a course,—conducting conferences, reading examination papers, and generally making himself useful at the instructor's behest. Thus at Harvard in 1897–8 eight such assistants were employed in the teaching of History and Government. Having taken the doctorate, such a man, if there happens to be room for him, may be engaged as an "Instructor" on a yearly tenure. The term "instructor," it must be explained, is used in Harvard in two senses : for every teacher in independent charge of a course, including the Professors; and also for the lowest grade of appointment to an independent charge. If he succeeds, the "Instructor" (in this latter sense) may be given an appointment for three years with the same title but with a seat in the " Faculty," which discusses all questions of curriculum and graduation.   The next stages are appointment as Assistant-Professor for five years ; a second appointment for the same term with a higher salary; and finally appointment as full Professor "without limit of term."   It needs no saying that this process is often greatly shortened, that instructors sometimes go elsewhere and are recalled to higher positions, and that professors are introduced from outside.   But in no case are vacancies advertised and testimonials invited : American scholars, like Scotch divines or German professors, have to wait for a " call."   In " extending " such "a call," or in granting promotion, the governing bodies are necessarily influenced by a number of considerations ; but one of the weightiest of these considerations is always the printed work of the available men.   In the bustling atmosphere of America the young assistant or instructor is so likely to become immersed in the details of examination and administration, that any circumstance is to be valued which reminds him that to save a little time for a piece of independent investigation may after all be his most prudent policy.

So far as the function of a university in the extension of knowledge is concerned, the academic situation is full of promise.   The chief source of anxiety is the condition of general culture.   But this is mainly a matter for the schools ; and of them the present writer is not competent to speak.

Printed in the United States
By Bookmasters